Comments on Tom O'Connell's Books and Lectures

"Tom O'Connell connects with readers soul to soul...inspires...Tom's memoirs are written like novels."
--Jordan Rich, *WBZ News Radio 1030,* Boston

"It's the finest example of anyone writing on this subject."
--Don LaTulippe, *WPLM Radio*, Plymouth

"Your talk was warm and funny...You are a natural storyteller."
--Shirley Eastman, *Friends of the Cotuit Library*

"A page turner...mind boggling...a stunning view."
--Melora North, *Cape Cod Magazine*

"O'Connell writes compellingly."
--Melanie Lauwers, *Cape Cod Times*

"Thank you for your delightful presentation."
--Justine Bowen, *Irish American Club of Cape Cod*

"Very vivid...A fascinating read."
--Bob Silverberg, *Books & The World TV*

"Thank you for your delightful presentation...warmly received."
--Kathie Glynn, *Falmouth Public Library*

"Earthy dialogue sprinkled with wit, candor and affection."
--*The Dedham Times*

Quotes from the pages of
Upward & Downward Mobility: *A Work Memoir*
(A Writer's Zigzag Journey)
by Tom O'Connell

As caddies, we were a bit invisible as we walked the course. It was the same kind of invisibility that wait staffs in restaurants and photographers enjoy. People forget they exist and are likely to say things intended to be private. (32)

After months of trying to sell the shampoo, I was left with a new basket on my bike, several unsold bottles of shampoo, and a financial loss. The whole experience was a dud. This was the first of many life lessons about the consequences of attempting to do something I was not cut out for. (35)

This was my first summer of total freedom and age 14 became an extended rite of passage. As one of the youngest caddies, I experienced an adolescent training program of sorts, especially in the barracks that housed us. (38)

At Massachusetts Osteopathic Hospital in Boston I served as a part-time custodian, working on weekends and holidays. When the full-time workers were elsewhere, I was waxing and buffing floors in patients' rooms and in the corridors. In addition, one of my functions there was to carry surgical leftovers to the incinerator. (60)

The refrigerator was ancient and didn't do a very good job of keeping its contents cold. So the hot dogs tended to have a gray coating on them which we would have to wash off before frying on the greasy grill. Since that time I have had a trust issue when it comes to hot dogs. (63)

Although jobs were scarce, I was able to find one at the Boston Envelope Company, about a mile from Granny's house on Walnut Place…One day when I arrived at work I found that the freight elevator had plunged from the top floor to the bottom of the elevator shaft. The wooden floor of the empty elevator had been shattered beyond recognition. (52)

We did a lot of drinking and worked hard as we framed in a whole house. I am still amazed as I reflect back on how the two of us, with him in the lead, framed a house from the foundation to the top of the roof in seven days. This included shingling the roof and installing the windows. (65)

The Army also provided some training that has been very useful throughout my adult life. I learned to touch type while I was with the Army's only Military Government (MG)

Group at Camp Gordon, Georgia. Also, I gained some useful experience as feature editor of our little MG newspaper. (79)

My job was to insert the tips of hundreds of cylinders of glass, one at a time, against a rapidly moving abrasive belt over which water flowed…the abrasive liquid flowed over the portion of my right hand between my index and middle fingers, causing a skin irritation that remained with me long after I left the job. (83)

Between the auto accidents and the wide variety of home owners' claims, it is no exaggeration to say that working for Amica always held my interest. I cannot think of many jobs that would expose a person to just about every aspect of modern civilization. Mine was that job. (92)

The salary was substantially less and I lost the benefit of a company car…But it was a trade-off I was willing to make. After all, I was moving toward a position that involved writing, my first love. As for the headaches of working a nine-to-five job five days a week, I entered a state of denial about that. (98)

When the directors held the meeting to vote on my acceptance I assumed that the vote would be unanimous in my favor. "All those in favor?" "Aye." It sounded like the whole group had responded in the affirmative.

"All those opposed?" When the query came for the "No" vote, a loud voice boomed out an emphatic "No!" (107)

At the eleventh hour, just before Christmas, the phone call came. They had decided to hire me. My position would start effective January 1, 1969, and I would be the Crum & Forster Claims Representative for Maine and New Hampshire, operating out of Portland. (132)

In my role as Executive Director, I reported to a large and unwieldy board of forty-two directors of varying ethnicity who represented the many public housing projects sprinkled throughout the city. There were so many minority folks on my board, I recall feeling embarrassed that I was so white. (136)

In the lobby outside the Governor's office on another occasion I was in a TV interview I have never forgotten. Dick Flavin, a veteran TV newscaster in Boston was interviewing me and he asked a very long question. (144)

Midway through the 1970s my mental state was in jeopardy because my work as Chief Executive of a prestigious organization seemed to be a pressure cooker constantly on the verge of exploding. (15)

When I was at the height of my mass media visibility, the President of the *Boston Globe Newspaper Company*, John Giuggio, approached me at a meeting we were attending and noted the extent to which I had become a public figure…He asked, "Would you be interested in running for Governor?" (156)

The show was approved, I got the green light, and we were launched based on this statement: "We'll try it for thirteen weeks." We produced two shows at a time twice a month and "It's Your Life" ran on Channel 25 every Sunday evening for nearly three years. (183)

Both the part-time teaching position plus the tutoring and advising for the Coaches & Mentors Program were destined to run for about 20 years. But I didn't think this conflicted with my pledge never to stay in the same full-time occupation more than five years. (203)

"Tom connects with readers soul to soul…inspires"
--Jordan Rich, *WBZ News Radio*, Boston

Upward & Downward Mobility

A Work Memoir
(A Writer's Zigzag Journey)

Tom O'Connell

Sanctuary Unlimited
www.sanctuary777.com

Upward & Downward Mobility:
A Work Memoir
(A Writer's Zigzag Journey)
by Tom O'Connell

Published in the United States by
Sanctuary Unlimited
P.O. Box 25, Dennisport, MA 02639
info@sanctuary777.com

This is a work of nonfiction.
All rights reserved, including the right of reproduction in whole or in part in any form. No part of this book may be used or reproduced in any form or by any means without permission in writing from the publisher except for brief quotes embodied in articles or reviews.

This book was printed in the United States of America.

To order additional copies of this book, contact your bookseller and refer to Ingram Book Company or go to amazon.com or Sanctuary Unlimited's sanctuary777.com.

Copyright 2013 Tom O'Connell
ISBN: 978-0-9827766-1-2

Thanks
To the God of Love and Truth and
to all those who have helped me to find my way through various life passages, challenging transitions, endurance tests, and intriguing mazes during this adventurous journey that we call life.

Note: Underneath each chapter heading I have included a very brief quotation from the amazing book *God Calling* by A.J. Russell. This is one of the most inspiring books I have ever owned. I have read from it daily through many years and have benefited greatly. (Barbour Publishing....www. barbour books.com)

A Sanctuary Unlimited Book

Upward & Downward Mobility:
A Work Memoir (A Writer's Zigzag Journey)
By Tom O'Connell   64,000 words   1930s to 2012

In a candid, informal style, writer Tom O'Connell traces his work life from his early days in the 1930s and 1940s as an orphan in a Catholic Charities group home upward to top leadership roles in Massachusetts. He recalls challenging careers as CEO, educator, writer, columnist, host of public affairs show "It's Your Life" on Boston's Channel 25.

People known nationally and locally emerge in this book: Victor Borge, John Volpe, Mike Dukakis, Dick Flavin, Paul Szep, Frank Sargent, Kevin White, Dapper O'Neil.

The memoir takes the reader on a roller coaster ride of job searches and major achievements as he moves upward from Granny's house next to the railroad tracks to appointment to the Governor's Highway Safety Committee, CEO of Massachusetts Safety Council, inclusion in *Who's Who in the East*, and selection in *Cape Cod Life's* 25th Anniversary Issue as "one of the top 100 influential people" on Cape Cod.

From heights of upward mobility and success, O'Connell also reveals periods when he plummeted from those heights into times of downward mobility when faced with divorce, illness, bankruptcy and other serious challenges.

"Tom re-creates the 'Anything is Possible' myth of American culture after World War II." --W. A. Cole, Book Reviewer

"This is more than a lone wolf's professional journal. His long time readers know Tom's independent thinking and deep faith. It's the story of a soul who will not sacrifice his values."
--Dr. Finbarr Corr, Author, Former Priest, Therapist, Professor

"Tom's memoirs are written like novels."
--Jordan Rich, *WBZ News Radio* 1030, Boston.

CONTENTS

1. Emotional & Mental Factors 13
2. A Perfectionist Training Program 17
3. Teenage Freedom & Work 38
4. Work and Life With My Irish Granny 42
5. Working My Way Through College 58
6. Dropping Out of B.C. & Transition Jobs 71
7. The U.S. Army & More Transition Jobs 78
8. Automobile Mutual Insurance Company 86
9. Public Information at Safety Council 97
10. CEO: Chevrolet Dealers Association 104
11. Writing & Politics & Maine Coast 120
12. Back to Claims Representative 131
13. CEO: Tenants Policy Council 136
14. CEO: Mass. Federation of Nursing Homes 142
15. CEO: Massachusetts Safety Council 152
16. Freelance Writer, Lecturer, Educator 165

Epigraphs

"You will come to know the truth and the truth will set you free."
–Jesus The Christ

"Be still and know that I am God."
--Psalm 46

"The face of truth remains hidden behind a circle of gold. Unveil it, O God of light, that I who love the true may see!"
--Isa Upanishad

"To different minds, the same world is a hell, and a heaven."
--Ralph Waldo Emerson

"It is at once our loneliness and our dignity to have an incommunicable personality that is ours, ours alone and no one else's, and will be so forever."
 --Thomas Merton

Upward & Downward Mobility:
A Work Memoir
(A Writer's Zigzag Journey)
by Tom O'Connell

1.
EMOTIONAL & MENTAL FACTORS
Bury every fear of the future (God Calling)

Introduction

Some people love to work. Others hate it. As for me, during much of my life I've had what I call an inconsistent relationship with work. Sometimes I thought of my work as interesting and fulfilling. Other times I considered work as a necessary evil that intruded into my creative life as a writer. Seldom have I been neutral in my thinking about work.

The word "work" can be defined in many ways. A job. An undertaking. An occupation. A duty. A task. I think of work as effort designed to accomplish a goal. For the sake of this book let's keep the word "effort" in our minds.

Work is an important survival skill and we need to learn how to work effectively. After all, most of us have to work to provide our food, clothing and shelter. That's the way it has been with me during most of my life.

Perhaps my survival skills, mostly self-taught, will help you to get some perspective on your own work life. Come to think of it, maybe you can borrow the title of the Boston area TV show I created and apply it to yourself. If you take "It's Your Life" and change the middle word, your own personal slogan becomes "It's My Life." That's a good slogan.

To explain successes and challenges I have experienced in my work life, I think the best approach is to start with a few of the conclusions experts came up with in May 1976 at the Lahey Clinic in Boston when I was 44 years old.

My attending physician and a Lahey psychiatrist were trying to understand my possibly "psychosomatic" physical disturbances and my mental tendency toward anxiety and depression. So I was asked to perform the intensive Minnesota Multiphasic Personality Inventory (MMPI).

The MMPI is a frequently used personality test in the field of mental health. The following gives you some of the highlights from my MMPI results and the psychiatric evaluation that followed a few weeks later:

- Highly rebellious and nonconformist
- Touchy, sensitive
- Artistic, bohemian temperament

- Confused feelings, moody
- Moderately depressed, worrying
- Restless or agitated

How would you like to have a person with these characteristics working for you? Or be your boss? Or better still, how would you like to have these characteristics and be your own boss? I have worked as employee, boss, and my own boss. It has been an interesting adventure.

When I first read my medical file and found the results, I thought they had exaggerated. But now, as I review my work life in this memoir I don't find much of a problem with the report. After all, the late 1960s, the 1970s, and the early 1980s were a horrendous time in my occupational, emotional and relationship life. I'm lucky I survived those years.

My marriage was steadily deteriorating as it moved inexorably toward nonexistence. My physical exhaustion was so intense that my body felt as if its component parts might be literally disintegrating. There were times on the sidewalks and streets of Boston when I felt weighted down like a deep sea diver. Other times my head felt light and my feet didn't even feel as if they were touching the ground.

Midway through the 1970s my mental state was in jeopardy because my work as Chief Executive of a prestigious organization seemed to be a pressure cooker constantly on the verge of exploding.

Also, my emotional state was in jeopardy because the fiction writing I had dedicated so much energy to for decades was not selling. Obviously, my mind was not pleased with the way I was living my life. So these factors were all reflected in the way I had replied to the MMPI questions.

In June 1976, one result of the psychiatric evaluation was a prescription for 10 mg. of Librium which was later changed to Valium. Also, it was suggested that I modify my behavior, find new ways of operating, reduce tension, and engage in a "program of moderation."

I was advised to "return to the primitive." Really? I thought life was about becoming more civilized, successful, and spiritual. However, on the spiritual side, the evaluation did recommend meditation "in brief spurts." Also, I was advised not to get too much rest: "Active diversion is better." On the whole, I think I got some useful advice.

But I'm getting a little bit ahead of myself here. We need to go back to the beginning of my work life. Forgive me when I go off on tangents. Although I'm aware that a certain amount of order in my life is helpful, I rebel at excessive structure. There's something very unnatural about it. Perhaps it reminds me too much of life at Mrs. White's house.

2.
A PERFECTIONIST TRAINING PROGRAM
Unseen forces are controlling your destiny (God Calling)

Mrs. White's Catholic Charities Home

My work memories begin at Mrs. White's house. Yes, that's what we called the place. It was not an orphanage. So we weren't called "orphans." It was not officially known as a foster home. So we weren't called "foster kids." In the current era the place might be called a group home.

In those days during the Great Depression prior to World War II it was simply "the White house" in the Boston suburb of Norwood, Massachusetts, where Margaret Monahan White, an Irish widow with one son who was a young adult, was in full control of the six boys in her temporary custodial care and answered to nobody but God, as far as I knew.

I guess once in a while she also answered to a social worker from the Catholic Charitable Bureau of the Boston area where she got the six of us boys from "broken homes," as they used to say. But most of the details of that part of my life have already been described in my book *The O'Connell Boy: Educating The Wolf Child~~an Irish-American Memoir (1932-1950).*

The short version of why I was being raised in a Catholic Charities home is simply that my mother had descended into a postpartum depression and other mental complications after my extremely difficult birth and she never recovered. Margaret lived the rest of her life in insane asylums and I never knew her or any Hendersons on her side of the family.

To complicate matters, at the age of six months I had a life-threatening experience with illness. I lost half my body weight and one of my lungs collapsed. But according to my father, Children's Hospital in Boston restored me.

Then tragedy struck again when I was two years old. My only sibling, my good natured little brother Jackie, was a year old when he died of pneumonia on my second birthday.

At the time, the two of us were in separate temporary homes. During my earliest years I was bounced around from one temporary care situation to another like a piece of baggage that had a confusing destination tag.

When I was about four or five I was living with Granny O'Connell and my father. Then, dramatically, at age five and a half I was deposited by my father at Mrs. White's house where I was destined to stay for nine years with five other boys of different ages. She always took six boys.

Enough about that. My focus in this current book is on my work history, with some other details that seem relevant.

Actually, "work" was an important word at Mrs. White's house. I'm surprised that Mrs. White's middle name wasn't "Work." She believed in work with religious conviction, or maybe it should be called fanaticism.

It's no exaggeration to say that she was an extreme perfectionist. I learned during many years of writing about mental health issues that perfectionism is a legitimate psychological disorder. She could have been the prototype.

Not only can perfectionism be seen as a psychological disorder, I link it to Obsessive-Compulsive Personality Disorder (OCD). And I call it a Don Quixote pursuit.

In real life, rigid order tends to be followed by chaos and vice-versa. However, in Mrs. White's house at 42 Mountain Avenue in Norwood, chaos was forbidden. There was a place for everything, and during the years I spent there, from age five in 1937 to age fourteen in 1946, everything was supposed to be in its assigned place. That included us boys.

"Didn't I tell you to be back here to the house by four o'clock?" "But we…" Whack! "We had to…" Whack! "We thought…" Whack! I'm surprised our brains were not completely dislodged from our skulls because of all the whacking. Maybe they were.

Excuses were not allowed in the White house. It was a house based on a simple philosophy of opposites. Black and white. Good and bad. "Yes, please" or "No, thank you." Seldom were shades of gray permitted.

Complaints were not allowed. And rules were not broken. She was more strict than a female Moses would have been. Every sentence she uttered to us was a commandment.

If there is one word to describe the most important reality in the White house it is the word "order." Our "guardian," as she was described on all official documents such as our report cards, had a process and a time for every function.

The sacrament of Confession, a mandatory weekly ritual, was held on Saturday afternoons in the little chapel to the rear of St. Catherine's with its entrance on Nahatan Street. Sunday was the Lord's Day and attendance at St. Catherine of Siena Roman Catholic Church was not optional.

At the age of five, when I arrived at 42 Mountain Avenue in Norwood, Massachusetts, I was soon introduced to the Mass and Sunday School even though we did not receive our First Communion until age seven.

Mrs. White's Orderly Life

On the home front, much of Mrs. White's orderly life was dedicated to maintaining a spic-and-span domicile. We boys functioned as her cleaning assistants. She was the worker-in-chief and was always too busy working to simply sit around.

The only time I ever saw her resting was for a short while on Sunday afternoons.

In my early weeks with her, my first introduction to work was simply to follow her orders and obey. "Get four large turnips in the cellar and bring them to the set tubs down there." Set tubs? What are they? I was afraid to ask.

I had learned right away that she hated questions. So I furtively whispered my questions to one of the other boys and learned that the set tubs were large soapstone sinks in the cellar that were used as part of the laundering process.

The ringer washer stood near the sinks. Also, there was a shelf holding large yellow bars of Kirkman's Soap. And there was a rustic toilet with a pull chain there for use by us boys during the daytime. We were only permitted to use the toilet in the second floor bathroom at or after bedtime.

Time was important to her and it was never to be wasted. She allocated days of the week to high priority activities such as church, laundry, ironing, vacuuming, and baking.

My favorite day was Saturday which was baking day. Except for the fact that we had to do chores in the morning and go to Confession in the afternoon, it was usually an enjoyable day that included a movie at the Norwood Theatre.

On baking day she made everything from scratch which was very labor intensive. No shortcuts for Mrs. White. She was not the type to seek easy ways to accomplish tasks. And her way was always the indisputable right way.

She had a very strong mind that held very strong opinions. She wouldn't even consider buying "store bread" because she looked on it with contempt, especially Wonder Bread. I don't think she viewed soft mass-produced store bread as real bread. She was probably right, considering the additives used to keep it soft and give it a longer shelf life.

Symbolizing her priorities, she had two pantries off the kitchen. One was for the sink, dishes, pots and pans. The other included many shelves filled with cooking supplies, Monarch brand canned goods, and boxes of food products such as Quaker Oats and Cream of Wheat.

Also in that pantry without a sink, she kept a full-sized barrel filled with white flour. There were sheet metal flour sifters there too to get the flour to the consistency she demanded. Whenever I was ordered to do some sifting I found it to be a very monotonous job. And the cloud of flour dust made me sneeze violently.

It was no random thing, the way I just used the word "ordered" in the previous paragraph. Mrs. White, a strong self-described "stout" woman with amazing strength and a massive reservoir of energy, was in charge of all she surveyed and delivered orders like a Commander-in-Chief.

Appointed by some distant unseen higher authority to rule and regulate the six of us boys, she did it as if she were the warden of a small prison or a military commander waging an important campaign.

Because she did nothing in a small way, her baking on Saturdays was a kind of campaign too. She baked white bread and raisin bread. And there was bread pudding too, either vanilla with raisins or plain chocolate. Sometimes she made both kinds.

Also, there was Irish soda bread with caraway seeds. I didn't like it because the seeds got stuck between my teeth. However, I liked her Irish bread, which was similar to the soda bread but without caraway seeds.

Today when I visit the Great Island Bakery on Cape Cod I only buy the Irish soda bread without the seeds. But when Mrs. White organized a household she seldom used a democratic process that included choices.

This did not mean we never had choices. It meant that choices were rarely offered by our esteemed guardian, the reigning monarch, the military dictator.

For example, at Easter she would let us choose between duck eggs and chicken eggs which could be boiled, fried or scrambled. And if you were foolish enough to ask for some other kind of egg you might find yourself getting no egg at all or a whack across your face with "the back of me hand."

No rebellion of any kind was permitted in her domain. Not even a hint of it. From her point of view I think questions were acts of rebellion so, as I've noted before, we boys seldom asked questions. And backtalk was forbidden.

Obviously, we learned to be good listeners and to this day I have that quality which is useful in close relationships and was helpful as an insurance claims investigator, journalist, Chief Executive, and freelance writer.

Back to the story about work. At Mrs. White's house there was always plenty of work to do. It was a large house, neat and orderly outside and inside, with two and a half stories, including the "finished room" on the third floor next to the unfinished attic. It was built according to Mrs. White's specifications before her husband died.

The younger three of the six boys, comprised of me and the two Rothwell brothers, slept up there in the finished room, two of us in the double bed and one in a cot near the dormer window occupied by the oldest boy, Joe Rothwell.

On the second floor there were three bedrooms and a bath. One of the bedrooms was occupied by Mr. Charles Vincent, the bachelor who roomed at Mrs. White's house during all the years I lived there. It was common in the 1930s and '40s for people to take in "boarders" who got their own bedroom and meals plus the use of kitchen and bath.

Mrs. White had her own very private bedroom and I'm unable to sort out how many boys shared the third bedroom on that floor. I just can't visualize how Bob Resker and Richard Roy and one or two young newcomers fit in there, along with her adult son, Tom, when he was around.

To avoid name confusion, Tom White was called Big Tom and I was called either Little Tom or "the O'Connell boy." Or if she happened to be angry at me I became Thomas O'Connell. Or even Thomas Frederick O'Connell, Junior.

In addition, there could be one or two young Irish immigrants in the house who might stay for a year or two on their way to becoming citizens. Malachy and Ted Kelliher did that. Somehow it all functioned well because Mrs. White managed to fit the placement puzzle together.

As for the work around the house, one example was cleaning the heavy wooden storm windows. The panes had to be cleaned inside and outside to the point that you wouldn't know there was any glass there.

We used clean pieces of old bed sheets and as we sprayed the Windex before wiping we were instructed to use plenty of "elbow grease" which was a phrase that meant absolutely nothing to me at the age of five. It made no more sense than the phrase "This will stick to your ribs" when applied to eating beef stew and dumplings.

We raked the gravel in the driveway so the lines would be parallel, and we raked the grass so it would be neat. Typically, Saturday began with vacuuming in the morning and we would carefully dust the mahogany furniture.

Also, on our knees we would comb the fringes of the Persian rugs in the "front room" and dining room. There were supposed to be no snarls in the fringes and they had to be parallel. Absolutely no snarls. Absolutely parallel.

Based on her fanaticism about the fringes on the rugs, maybe some of her perfectionism could be described as parallelism. This would be a peculiar subcategory of her obsessive-compulsive disorder.

Mrs. White was never satisfied with half measures. All tasks had to be done to perfection, including how well we polished our footwear. The goal was to see your face in your leather shoes.

To help facilitate this, we boys went to Winslow Brothers & Smith tannery on nearby Railroad Avenue by the railroad tracks a short walk from Mountain Avenue. There we begged the men on the loading docks for scraps of sheepskin. Used for buffing our leather shoes, these scraps provided the ultimate shine along with a pleasant leather scent.

If she had performed a different role in life, Mrs. White

could have easily handled being a queen, a general, or even a Marine Corps officer in charge of training drill sergeants. Royal or military precision would have been easy for her.

Looking back, I sometimes think of her as Snow White, but instead of seven dwarfs she had six of us boys. As an instant work crew, we were readily available for any kind of task such as painting the outside of the house.

Like the seven dwarfs, we had a varied assortment of personalities. And she used us according to our ages. No boy was ever exempt from work. When we were not working we were studying, and at certain approved times we were at the kitchen table playing board games such as Monopoly or Checkers.

Also, we might be sent outdoors as a group to play baseball at the field on the next street called White's Field which was her own empty house lot. Her large house had been built on a very small lot with a tiny back yard. But her additional lot was only a couple of minutes away. Its purpose was never explained, just as most things were not explained.

As I've noted already, questions were unwelcome in Mrs. White's house. And explanations to us boys were rare. In those days the common belief was that kids needed no explanations about life. The two rules for most children were "Do what you're told" and "Be seen and not heard."

For unsupervised entertainment, we had "the woods" at the end of Mountain Avenue. There we risked our lives and our limbs with escapades we invented. Also, the woods gave us a plentiful supply of high-bush blueberries that we usually sold to Gertrude's Pastry Shoppe on Washington Street for muffins and pies. If Gertrude's didn't need our berries we tried Lewis' Restaurant near the Norwood Theatre.

For plump low-bush blueberries we took a very long hike to O'Toole's sand pits on the other side of Route One near the section of Westwood called Islington. Trudging back toward home across Route One and along Pleasant Street near my Cornelius M. Callahan public elementary school, the berries would settle a little.

But we found that shaking the bottle or jar the right way could get the container to look full again. Sometimes I would wonder if this might be dishonest, but then I would remind myself that the jar was full at the start of my trek home and I was just returning it to its original state.

During elementary school I had a paper route for a while, delivering the weekly *Norwood Free Press* door to door. It wasn't hard work, and I tried to be honest about it. Although there was a temptation to take bundles of the papers and dump them into a culvert instead of delivering them, I chose the legitimate delivery process.

At a very young age, Mrs. White allowed us to caddy at Norfolk Golf Course in Westwood a few miles from our house in Norwood. To get there we would bicycle along Washington Street and then eventually pedal over the bridge at Route One and up a long hill to the Golf Course.

Often we would park our bikes in Norwood at the old cemetery off Railroad Avenue and we would hitchhike to the golf course. That was a bit of adventure in its own right. We never told Mrs. White that we thumbed rides and she never asked. So she probably knew.

Next we'll take a look at my work as a caddy but more details of life at the caddy shack and other aspects of my early life are found in *The O'Connell Boy: Educating the Wolf Child~An Irish-American Memoir (1932-1950)*.

Norfolk Golf Course & The Caddy Shack

The caddy shack at Norfolk Golf Course was the focal point of a young lifestyle that included a vast array of experiences, some of them life-threatening or possibly threatening to one's sense of self.

The shack was located to the rear of the club house which was the members' domain. The club house was not to be entered by a caddy without special permission.

To understand the caddy shack, picture an oblong bit of

earth resembling a patio and elevated several feet above the slope of a steep hill on the fifth hole, with a stone wall supporting it and a lattice-walled shelter on top of the flattened pile of earth that served as a dirt floor.

Three walls were lattice. The fourth was the club house. You might say we caddies were loosely connected to the club house. Also, we had a flat tarpaper roof to protect us from the weather while we awaited our assignments.

One of the corners of the shack against the club house was called "piss corner" and it served that purpose. They certainly weren't going to let us use the club house facilities. And I don't recall any plumbing for drinking water or any other use in the caddy shack.

Since the urine had no place to go except into the compacted earth that served as the floor of the shack, there was always a urine smell in that space next to the club house. The smell tended to be more pervasive on humid days despite the ventilation provided by the lattice. If defecation was needed, there were woods surrounding the course.

Against the latticed walls were lengthy built-in wooden benches where we would sit according to seniority that was decided by the boys who had been caddying the longest. It was an exercise in self-government with a touch of tyranny.

There was no formal supervision in the caddy shack

despite the existence of a man described as the "caddy master" who operated from the main club house at a distance from us and called out your name when it was your turn to work. "O'Connell to the first tee!"

Also in the club house, there was a pro shop with a professional golfer known as "the pro." When the pro was not giving lessons, he managed the shop and lived in a rarified atmosphere that commanded respect while keeping him a bit secluded. The "members" who populated that building were treated like royalty because they paid hefty dues to keep the whole enterprise going.

When I was initiated into life at the caddy shack I was probably about ten years old. Those of us who were newcomers and not very muscular were given golfers with light white canvas bags holding just a few clubs. We caddied "singles" and received 75 cents for eighteen holes. Since Norfolk was a nine-hole course, the nine holes had to be completed twice to equal eighteen.

As we got older we carried "doubles" which meant a bag on each shoulder and, of course, double the pay. I never enjoyed doubles. Not just because of the heavier weight and the straps digging into my bony shoulders, but also because I would have to keep track of what both golfers were doing.

I would need to know where their balls went, and I had to

keep scooting from one golfer to the other to provide the right club for each shot, while trying not to delay the movement of the foursome or twosome along the fairway.

I was not born with hurrying as a part of my nature and I have always hated being pressured to do things faster. Obviously, I have never considered speed a virtue. That's why the gym teacher in Norwood Junior High always called me Old Man O'Connell. The more he called me that the slower I got. Now I am actually an old man and finally fit his description more accurately.

In spite of my speed deficit, I caddied at Norfolk Golf Course throughout most of the nine years at Mrs. White's. It was pretty good work except on roasting hot days or when rain couldn't be avoided.

Most of the golfers were kind to us and usually gave us a tip. Instead of the 75 cent basic fee they would give us a dollar or even more. But there was a legend at Norfolk about the member who was a Scottish chauffeur for one of the millionaire Endicotts in Dedham. The Scot gave a caddy 74 cents and a stick of gum. In those days a pack of gum cost five cents, making a stick worth a penny.

As caddies, we were a bit invisible as we walked the course. It was the same kind of invisibility that wait staffs in restaurants and photographers enjoy. People forget they exist and are likely to say things intended to be private.

While the golfers talked to each other, we would quietly observe just about every kind of golfer temperament ranging from fury when a shot went into the rough and on down the scale to disappointment verging on tears when a ball landed in a sand trap with a large overhanging lip.

There were bursts of happiness too when a ball landed on the green and rolled to a point a couple of feet from the pin. "Now that was a golf shot," the proud golfer or one of his pals would say.

People took their golf game very seriously. Sometimes too seriously. I recall one instance of anger from a robust businessman who got so full of purple-faced rage that he actually wrapped his club around a tree. His drive on the par three third hole had not met his high expectations.

As for the language he used, it was not the kind spoken at Mrs. White's where no vulgarity was allowed. He used caddy shack language. Usually, the public language on the golf course at Norfolk was polite and civilized.

Golf in those times was primarily a men's game and few women were members there. So golf was considered a "gentleman's game." Swearing, although tolerated, was not considered gentlemanly.

In those days it was standard to train a boy to become a

gentleman. But we don't use the word "gentleman" much today. I don't know why. But I've come to believe that we each have saintly and devilish spirits affecting our behavior. My own devilish spirit sometimes uses very earthy Anglo-Saxon language. Caddy shack language. Words to avoid.

As I grew older at Norfolk Golf Course and became more of a free spirit, even an entrepreneur of sorts, I would often avoid caddying and hunt for golf balls instead. I would patrol the roughs and out-of-bounds areas in my quest for lost balls that had a good resale value. Titleists were always a great find and I had no trouble locating buyers.

There were hazards when hunting for balls. One was poison ivy and another was the presence of snakes or black widow spiders. In those days we heard stories of rattlesnakes being seen in the Blue Hills which could be viewed from Westwood if you had the right vantage point.

We didn't have to stretch our imaginations far to think the rattlers might be in any part of the woods, especially in stone walls like the one that ran along the second hole at Norfolk.

Each time we decided to reach a hand into a hole in the earth or into the space between rocks in a wall, this action brought a sudden burst of fear. The sight of a snake, even a harmless garter snake, always triggered an instant panic.

Oh yes, I almost forgot about the bees. The woods and

fields surrounding the golf course had bushes of all types and often we would start poking around the blueberry bushes without scanning for bees' nests. The results could be very painful. For example, there was the time Joe Rothwell disturbed a nest of bees while he was urinating and got stung in the gonads. He was much more cautious after that.

Other Employment While at Mrs. White's

Coming across a classified ad one time when I was in junior high school, I found what seemed to be a good opportunity to make some money without working hard. It was one of those "self-starter" ads about selling shampoo.

To sell the product I needed to buy a basket for my Columbia bicycle and invest money up front to obtain a supply of shampoo. I saved up and bought two cartons of the product with a dozen bottles in each box.

After months of trying to sell the shampoo, I was left with a new basket on my bike, several unsold bottles of shampoo, and a financial loss. The whole experience was a dud.

This was the first of many life lessons about the consequences of attempting to do something I was not cut out for. As a shy introvert I definitely was not the type to go "cold calling" on prospects and try to sell them a product they did not need.

Selling chances on 50 gallons of heating oil to raise money for St. Catherine's Parish was a different story. My shyness was not a hindrance and people responded enthusiastically to that kind of fund raising campaign.

Another work adventure during junior high school was when I agreed to substitute for my friend John Flaherty during a couple of summer weeks when he took time off from his part-time bakery job at Gertrude's Pastry Shoppe.

The job was washing pots and pans in a huge sink with strong soap. I have never forgotten the unholy mess that emerged in the bakery after the baking was done. The dough stuck like cement to the sides of the baking pans.

The combination of intense heat from the huge baking ovens and heat from the soapy steaming hot water in the sink was about enough to put me in a catatonic state. I've always been allergic to extreme heat. The days seemed very long and I was greatly relieved when John returned.

From time to time I also served as a pin boy at the Sports Center bowling alley. This was before the days when pin setting machines were automated. We had to set up the candle pins manually. Unfortunately, some bowlers used us as targets in the few seconds between setting up the pins and leaping up from the pit to a safer place. In that gap a bowler night prematurely heave the ball down the alley, smash the pins and send them flying like projectiles. So I had to learn to be a skilled dodger.

Naturally, it didn't take long before I decided not to do that kind of work. I preferred to keep my body from being wounded. Also, I was not much for dodging and leaping. But the time would soon come when my work would require a minimum of dodging and no leaping.

I should also mention at this time that while I was living at Mrs. White's my interest in words was turning into an obsession that would affect my work choices as an adult.

In the six years of elementary school I won all the spelling bees. And in the fifth grade I wrote a prize-winning essay about our school's fund raising for the war effort. We had helped pay for the production of a World War II jeep.

When my story about our patriotic fund raising won the essay contest, it was published in the *Norwood Messenger*, the town's number one weekly newspaper. This planted a deep seated sense of destiny in my psyche about my need to eventually become a journalist.

Then, in junior high I became the feature editor of our school magazine, the *Junior Narrator*. Fortunately, as I grew, my love of reading and writing was encouraged at Mrs. White's. It was an important aspect of my essential personality and it would continue throughout my life.

3.
TEENAGE FREEDOM & WORK
Lose sight of all limitations (God Calling)

Saranac Inn in the Adirondacks

At age fourteen I finally left Mrs. White's house. My father's black '37 Plymouth had been brand new when he had taken me to 42 Mountain Avenue in Norwood. Now, in 1946 as we headed toward East Dedham and Granny's house near the railroad tracks and the decaying East Dedham Station, the car's paint had faded and the vehicle had added much mileage. My father and I had added much mileage too.

My few belongings, such as my *Webster's Dictionary* and a book on ancient history titled *Man's Great Adventure*, were placed on the back seat and a while later my stuff was deposited at Granny's soot speckled 22 Walnut Place duplex.

Without delay, I was off to South Station in Boston to connect with the Albany train and head for upstate New York to join Dave and Joe Rothwell, who had left Mrs. White's three years earlier. They were caddying at Saranac Inn in the Adirondacks and had made arrangements for me to join them in the caddy camp barracks for the summer.

This was my first summer of total freedom and age 14

became an extended rite of passage. As one of the youngest caddies, I experienced an adolescent training program of sorts, especially in the barracks that housed us.

Considering the sexual lower education I had already received in the caddy shack at Norfolk Golf Course, Saranac could be described as "continuing ed."

There was no real supervision in that barracks where one had to be careful not to offend the older boys, especially those from Utica and Syracuse, New York, who were very tough. They reminded me of the Dead End Kids of movie fame, and the Bowery Boys. I had observed many fist fights over the years, and had been in a few, but I had never seen such bloody battles as I saw at the caddy camp.

Drinking and gambling may not have been permitted there, but both were part of the way of life. That's when I had my first experience of drinking until I was very drunk. Looking back, I believe I had alcohol poisoning. It took me weeks to recover from the nonstop beer guzzling. Because it made me so ill I didn't drink alcohol again until after I had graduated from high school.

As for the gambling, I was a very poor loser. So I learned to bet "on the side" when other guys were gambling at cards or rolling dice, and I was able to win from time to time.

While at Saranac Inn I received my first Social Security

card which began with three digits in common with many New Yorkers, and that has accompanied me through life. This was the first period in my life when the flow of income enabled me to spend some money on good times.

At Saranac, I had my first experiences of horseback riding. I found it interesting until an independent stallion, alleged to be a mare, ran away with me. It refused to obey me as it raced around the trail near Saranac Lake through overhanging tree branches that whipped me as I passed.

To this day, I don't know how I stayed in the saddle until the horse chose to slow down. Eventually, it decided on its own to come to a stop near the stable and I don't recall much horseback riding after that experience.

I clearly remember one night as I was betting on the side at a card game, one of my friends suggested that I join him and a few others for a ride toward the Canadian border. I told him I wasn't interested because I was doing well at gambling. My choice turned out to be a healthy one.

Their car skidded off the road at high speed, crashing through trees and tumbling end over end several times. It came to rest in a swamp with the hot exhaust pipe pressing against the body of one of the guys. Those were the days when cars had no seat belts. The boys were all injured in a variety of ways and their sojourn at Saranac Inn was over.

When my own summer of freedom in the Adirondacks ended, I was pretty broke because we had gone on strike at the caddy camp and had been replaced by strike breakers. Other boys were ready and very willing to replace us. This taught me a good lesson about power in the workplace. We were expendable.

Having hung out with some local teenage girls at Lake Placid during the summer, I spent the last few weeks of August at a girl's house there. I asked the caddy camp to mail the rest of my pay to Granny's house in East Dedham.

At that point I had just enough money in my wallet for my Trailways bus fare from Lake Placid to Albany. From Albany, with a light wallet, I hitchhiked through the night to Massachusetts and Granny O'Connell's ancient duplex at 22 Walnut Place next to the East Dedham railroad station.

A brand new phase in my home life and work life was about to begin.

Note: The Walnut Place address no longer exists. The street was renamed Hazelnut Place and the house numbers were rearranged. They tampered with my personal history without asking for my permission.

4.

WORK AND LIFE WITH MY IRISH GRANNY

Be calm, no matter what (God Calling)

Work While Living with Granny in Dedham

At Granny's duplex in the fall of 1946 I swapped Mrs. White's perfectionism and discipline for the freedom to do pretty much as I pleased. My Irish Granny was an old woman and her child rearing days had ended decades before. Also, since my father was living there part of the time she didn't consider me to be her responsibility.

In truth, my father didn't think much about being responsible for me either. After all, I was fourteen years old and in my father's time that age had been considered early adulthood. Actually, his neglect was fine by me because freedom was so precious to me.

I think the craving for freedom may have been in the DNA of the O'Connells. My grandfather Dan O'Connell ran away from home at age fourteen, became a barber, and never looked back. And during my father's time with the Dedham Post Office he always dreamed of setting himself free.

The difference between Mrs. White's house and Granny's was dramatic. In the current era, my lifestyle at Mrs. White's might be described as "middle class." Actually, I have learned that in the '30s and '40s Catholic Charities was sometimes seen as an agency serving the middle class. By those standards, the move to Granny's ramshackle duplex on the wrong side of Dedham's tracks was a serious social and housing downgrade that brought with it near starvation.

Yet there was something about living next to the train station that I always found fascinating. From Granny's kitchen, without getting up from my seat at the kitchen table, I could watch the commuters arriving or departing. The men would have felt hats, umbrellas, and briefcases. The women would be dressed in their best attire.

There was an air of mystery at the East Dedham Station. It tended to look like a still life from the 19th Century. What would the passengers be doing in Boston? Would I some day be commuting by train to the city to fill an important job? My mind had a field day speculating.

Back to the housing downgrade. It was not a real problem for me. I was so happy to be free I was not likely to complain about what I lacked. As they say, beggars can't be choosers. However, I had enough brass to make wisecracks about the food deficit now and then. The food shortage was very extreme and my appetite was amazingly persistent.

When my father was around I didn't see much of him but

at least there was food in the house such as canned peas and diced carrots. He would buy a whole case of the same item with a case having 24 cans that would last nearly a month. Every so often, his selection would be the feast called Dinty Moore's Beef Stew which included protein, a nutrient that was usually hard to find in Granny's house.

She was not noted for her cooking skill, was uninterested in nutrition, and spent most of her time rocking in her old rocker muttering the prayers of her rosary. "All I need is a bit o' tea and toast," she would say. But I needed actual food.

I continued to caddy at Norfolk Golf Course which was no farther away than when I had lived in Norwood. The bike ride was not painful because there were few large hills other than the ones on which the golf course was located. In addition to caddying, now and then there were babysitting jobs with the families of uncles and aunts.

During high school I worked part-time at a soda fountain called The 400 in Dedham Square opposite the bicycle shop. During my shifts I could consume ice cream and other snacks such as Peggy Lawton's brownies. This helped offset the malnutrition I was experiencing at Granny's house.

I am not exaggerating about the malnutrition. Later in life when a chiropractor was examining my tongue he reeled off a number of phrases for diseases recorded there that were usually attributed to a lack of sound nutrition. A person's tongue is like a health diary. My scarred tongue to this day looks like a parched riverbed.

During the transition from Norwood to Dedham I commuted for a while to a couple of supermarket jobs in Norwood. One was with the First National store and the other with the A&P: the Atlantic and Pacific Tea Company.

The First National job found me stocking shelves with canned goods. The A&P used me as a "bundle boy" who filled bags with groceries at the checkout counter and sometimes lugged customers' groceries to their cars. I stopped that job when my feet became badly infected after some episodes of working in the rain with leaky shoes.

Downward Mobility in East Dedham

During the late 1940s and early 1950s I learned to live with the bare minimum of income and, in fact, the bare minimum of most things including food, clothing, and adequate shelter.

In those days we didn't have "the poverty level" and weren't conscious of where we stood in the class structure. You might say we were accustomed to living "on the edge" but didn't have a phrase to describe it.

East Dedham was considered to be on the lowest rung of

the economic ladder and the old Square was a short walk from Granny's duplex. But those who lived in East Dedham were usually proud of the area even though it contained more blighted houses than elsewhere. People in East Dedham certainly couldn't be accused of "putting on airs," as the Irish were accustomed to saying. They were down to earth folks.

I believe there were more saloons in the Square than in any other suburb of Boston. One of them was the Hartnett Square Social Club. The large panes of glass in its windows facing the street were painted black to give privacy to the customers inside the club. Outside you could use the plate glass windows as a full length mirror. As for social activities, I never found out about that aspect of the "Social Club."

The more middle class section of Dedham called Oakdale began on the other side of the tracks behind Granny's duplex. East Dedham Square itself was a throwback to an earlier grungy Dickensian time in history and was eventually replaced, courtesy of an urban renewal project.

Living so close to the Square, it was natural for me to gravitate to the decadent poolroom above the First National store. Curiosity was a strong part of my nature, and since the poolroom was the kind of place that was avoided by folks concerned with their reputations, that made it all the more interesting. My pals and I would often hang out at the poolroom because we weren't out to impress anybody.

Actually, our favorite corner in East Dedham Square, which had several corners, was the one where Gates Pharmacy was located. It had an excellent soda fountain, and somehow Doc Gates and the pharmacist who succeeded him gave us squatter's rights there. It became "our corner."

Across the Square was a corner occupied by tough guys. Typically, as I passed by I would hear one of them say, "Just got back from Bridgewater." In other words, he had just been released from prison, probably after an episode of public drunkenness which was against the law in those days.

Near that same corner was the headquarters of the East Dedham Improvement and Athletic Association, also known as "The I and A." It didn't stir up my curiosity. I know of no athletic events performed there, nor did it seem to make any improvements in the area before urban renewal. But I believe the club provided low cost alcohol for its members and a relaxed atmosphere for playing cards and other games.

Default on a Promise

In the spring of 1949, as I was finishing my senior year at Dedham High School where I was consistently on the Honor Roll, I received my acceptance letter from Boston College. This was a high point in my life. But when I told my father about it, he informed me that he had to default on his promise to pay my tuition.

My high point in life rapidly became a low point. Why did he fail to come through for me? He had other plans that were important to him. Prior to that, he had other plans when he had put me in a group home at age five.

When I was finished with elementary school and expected to move back to Granny's house with my father, again he had other plans. At that time he informed me of his decision to keep me at Mrs. White's until I completed ninth grade and could take care of myself after relocating to Granny's place.

I was often surprised and frustrated by his decisions. One of the worst letdowns was his behavior when I was entering my senior year at Dedham High School. I was eagerly looking forward to being a freshman at Boston College the following September and assumed I would be able to do that.

However, Fred and his girl friend Hazel chose that time to leave the security of their civil service jobs at Dedham Post Office. They moved to Wells, Maine to embark on a small business enterprise known as Brookland Motor Court.

Because of this venture, I was left at Granny's house while Fred took off with the money my grandmother told me she had set aside to help me begin college. Taking every dollar he could gather, he pooled his funds with Hazel's and they invested in construction of their new motor court on Route One in Wells near the Drakes Island Road.

This was accompanied by another of my father's periodic promises. At that time he said that some day I would benefit from the enterprise. But it never happened.

His frequent "disappearing acts" and unfulfilled promises left me shaking my head. Even though past experience had told me to be wary of his promises, I still tended to believe his assertions until they proved to be wanting.

Over the years it was obvious to me that involvement in my care was not at the top of my father's priority list. But I never thought of him as evil. At times he could be very generous. So the key word for him was "inconsistent."

Based on my father's inconsistency and his unpredictable actions when it came to my existence, I believe I have had a much greater resistance to authority figures than most people manifest. "Who said so?" "Oh really?" "Prove it."

On the one hand, deep disappointment became a way of life for me when I depended on Freddy. On the other hand, he would show great concern from time to time. And he could be very thoughtful. This left me off balance.

Could I develop a Buddhist detachment about his behavior? No. I found it disillusioning and depressing. Yet I would shrug my shoulders as I tried to cope with his tendency to minimize, maximize, or distort the truth. I would say to myself or a friend, "With Freddy, you have to divide by two or multiply by two when he makes a statement."

If he said he would come down from Maine and visit Granny and me in two months with a supply of food, I would assume he would come in four months. If he said he'd have a hundred dollars for me in the near future, I would assume he'd have fifty dollars.

Time after time, after receiving a promise from him I felt like a person who was guaranteed safe passage across a river near a waterfall and then given a leaky rowboat with no oars.

So you can imagine how I distrusted people's promises when I reached adult life and the world of work. I became a fanatic about my individual freedom and at the same time I distrusted anybody and everybody when it came to pledges and promises. It's good to be a bit skeptical but it was a burden to be a person who fundamentally distrusted others.

Nevertheless, the situation I found myself in with Freddy helped motivate me to maintain my excellent grades in high school and I also found time to prepare for the Boston Herald Traveler Spelling Bee. After reviewing massive sheets of paper listing thousands of possible words that might be asked, I won the contest at Dedham High and was declared School Champion. In the finals at Boston Public Library, however, I goofed on a fairly easy word. And that was that.

Working With My Father in Maine

During the summer after Dedham High School graduation in 1949 I accepted my father's invitation to live in Wells, Maine with him and Hazel for the season in a small cottage that doubled as the office structure for the developing "field" of cottages. Having started with 10 prefabricated cottages that spring, they were now adding two cottages to the field.

I played the role of "carpenter's helper" as my father measured, hammered and sawed while we assembled the two additional cottages, but I have no trouble admitting that I was not a very energetic helper. The kind of physical labor my father seemed to thrive on had never been one of my strong preferences. I was lazy physically and active mentally.

When the summer of 1949 was over, I returned to Granny's house in my 1934 Plymouth coupe that had been passed on to me by Hazel's brother. He had lost his driver's license for an indefinite period because of a serious infraction of the rules, and the old car had been in storage.

During my stay in Maine, my father had asked Hazel's unlicensed brother to teach me to drive. Ironically, I was living across the street from the Maine State Police barracks and being trained on Route One by an unlicensed driver. But he taught me very well. Hazel's other brother who had a legal license accompanied me to the driving test back in Norwood, Massachusetts. And I passed.

The Boston Envelope Company

My next step was to find a job for the fall of 1949 and then work and save up for a year to meet my tuition before entering Boston College in the fall of 1950. Although jobs were scarce, I was able to find one at the Boston Envelope Company, about a mile from Granny's house on Walnut Place. So I spent the year working at the factory that was one of suburban Dedham's few substantial industries.

There is a legend in Dedham about an attempt by the wealthy Endicotts to set up a major industry in that town. The controlling powers in town gave the project thumbs down, so the Endicotts took their idea to New York State where they founded the community of Endicott, New York. Then they developed the Endicott-Johnson Shoe Company.

Yet Wendell Endicott and Katherine his adopted sister maintained their mansions in Dedham. Wendell's showplace eventually became MIT's Endicott House. Although there was a move toward using the deceased Katherine's place as a Massachusetts Governor's Mansion, that failed. Instead, the property was given to the Town for a variety of civic uses. A few years ago I enjoyed giving a book presentation lecture there to the Dedham Retired Men's Club. It's an impressive setting and a mansion in the true sense of the word.

At any rate, at age seventeen I was having my first exposure to full-time work at the envelope company. My starting pay was 90 cents an hour. Because of Granny O'Connell's generosity I saved most of each week's pay while maintaining the old car. Throughout college Granny let me stay on her side of the duplex without requiring me to pay room and board. I have always been grateful for that.

When my bachelor Uncle Joe was working in Washington, D.C. I used his bedroom. At times when he came home for a vacation, I relocated myself from his room to the double bed in my father's bedroom.

Before my father moved to Maine I had to share his bed when Joe was around. Even after Freddy moved, his bed at 22 Walnut Place was still waiting for him. If he came down for a visit and Uncle Joe was in Washington I kept Joe's room. If Uncle Joe was at Granny's on one of his periodic visits I forfeited my privacy and shared my father's bed.

This perpetuated the feeling I had in earlier years at Mrs. White's of having no permanent sleeping location. I recall that in the scripture Jesus commented on having no fixed place to rest his head. He was a transient. So was I.

I learned at that fairly young age at Granny's place that when you have your own private bedroom even for a short time it's not easy to return to sharing a bedroom. I may have been a transient but I didn't necessarily like it.

However, despite questions about having my own bedroom, there was one thing I was certain about. I was determined to let nothing get in the way of my pursuit of a liberal arts education at Boston College starting a year later.

During my opening months at the Boston Envelope Company, I had my first experience of checking in and out with a time clock. My position was called "floor boy." With a device called a "jack" on metal wheels, my job was to jack up and pull loaded pallets of flat paper cut-outs to the folding machines where cut-outs were transformed into envelopes.

I also had to carry large glue buckets to keep the glue containers full at each machine. Later I would haul the folded and completed envelopes away after they were deposited in boxes of 500.

The envelope production process began with reams of paper, 500 sheets to a ream. They were hauled by another worker with a motorized jack from the loading platform area to a cutter who would work on a single ream at a time.

A cutter would take a steel die in the shape of an unfolded

envelope and slide it into a large press on top of a ream of paper. The operator was only allowed seconds to perform his insertion maneuver and swiftly yank his hands out of the way. Then the heavy press, slamming down with a quick crunch, would create stacks of 500 unfolded envelopes.

If the cutter was skillful and lucky, his fingers would remain intact. A mistake could lead to a serious finger or hand injury. I noticed one cutter's missing fingers. But this didn't seem to faze the cutter who had a high hourly rate compared to other workers. It was similar to receiving combat pay for hazardous duty in the military.

When enough piles were lined up on a pallet my job was to get them to one of the folding and gluing machines which were all operated by women. If their supply of paper became low or if it appeared that they were low on glue the women's voices would ring out above the clatter of the machinery.

They would yell "Floor boy!" or a few other choice words. That was where I learned that some women could be as vulgar and raunchy as the toughest guys.

Even though I was skinny and not very muscular, I could use leverage with a mechanical or hydraulic jack as I hoisted a wooden pallet with its thousands of sheets of paper or its packed boxes of completed envelopes.

Then the jack's steel wheels would help me transport the

envelopes to their next destination. Usually I would head upstairs by freight elevator to the mailing and shipping room. There were no hills to climb so the job was not as rigorous as it might have been.

One day when I arrived at work I found that the freight elevator had plunged from the top floor to the bottom of the elevator shaft. The wooden floor of the empty elevator had been shattered beyond recognition. But fortunately nobody was on the elevator at the time.

I considered myself lucky not to have been on the elevator in the daytime with a load when that mishap had happened. From then on I never felt quite safe on that elevator.

The floor boy was expected to be very reliable, and most of the time I was. But every so often I would make a large mistake. Sometimes the pallet I was pulling too fast would sway and many thousands of flat pieces of paper would go flying across the floor in slow motion, leading to a very embarrassing painfully slow cleanup.

I think this whole cutting and folding and gluing process on the envelopes' journey to the shipping room helped me to understand some of the process of lugging stones to erect pyramids in ancient Egypt. Repetitive and monotonous.

As for the envelopes that look so neat and clean when we buy them, I never since that time have licked an envelope. At first I used a sponge or a little spit to moisten the dried glue. Eventually, I graduated to glue sticks.

Factories today are probably much more sanitary, but in those days one could not be sure what might have found its way into the glue along with the highly visible insects. I had rare views of a production process that most people never saw. So I am an unabashed glue avoider. Why risk it?

Looking back, I can see that my work at the envelope factory was good training for adult life. As a factory worker I was part of a world within a world with its own structure. It functioned as a productive island in the middle of a vast nation of other structures with specialized functions.

The envelope itself could be found just about everywhere in civilization. And the transportation of envelopes through the mail and other means of delivery was vitally necessary to modern society in the era before emails and faxes.

The pay was not exceptional at the factory, but the work was steady and once you knew your job you were treated with respect. That was quite important to me.

Critically important was the fact that the Boston Envelope Company was providing the financial bridge I could trudge across to reach Boston College. And that was very good.

5.
WORKING MY WAY THROUGH COLLEGE
Never doubt. Have no fear (God Calling)

The Loan

In the spring of 1950 my personal master plan for higher education was coming along well. I had steady employment at the Boston Envelope Company, and got a pay raise when my boss Joe Venis promoted me to the shipping room on the second floor with its view of Mother Brook, perhaps the earliest canal in America. There I wrapped and addressed boxes of envelopes to be shipped around the United States.

Receiving steady work and steady pay, I was able to stick to my weekly saving schedule which gave me a sense of security by the time I had amassed most of my first year's tuition. It was a very good feeling.

Then came my father's visit from Maine with a request that gave me the horrors and intensified my anxiety level for years to come. My sense of security turned to an ongoing sense of insecurity. And I was part of the problem.

I still had not learned that it's hazardous to tell other people much about one's earnings or assets. I had told my father too much. Knowing I was diligently saving toward

Boston College, Fred asked me for a loan because in its second year the motor court in Maine was experiencing some serious financial challenges. He seemed desperate. And after all, in spite of his deficiencies he was my father.

I was faced with a dilemma because I had minimal trust in Fred's ability to honor an agreement. After all, he had abandoned me to a group home at age 5 and had recently broken his pledge to Mrs. White that he would help me launch my college education. Instead, due to his unreliable behavior I was becoming educated at the College of Hard Knocks while majoring in factory labor.

Here he was, appearing to be more of an adversary than a parent, and if I gave him my money I would be jeopardizing my ability to start off college with a sound financial basis. However, based on my Christian faith we were supposed to honor our parents. So I delayed my answer for a few days, and prayed about it.

Finally, I told him I'd let him borrow a substantial portion of my savings based on his promise to repay my loan in the fall. I had the wisdom to hold back enough in my savings account to get me started with the first semester's tuition and books, and loaned him the rest. My mistake.

Consistent with his tendency to default on promises, in the fall he didn't have the money to repay me as my freshman year was imminent. He said he had underestimated the costs of developing the new enterprise. So I had to wait…and wait.

Emotionally, I resembled the characters in the film *Casablanca* who kept looking skyward while hoping to get a rare seat on the solitary flight to Lisbon.

During my early years of college, my father was very slow to come through with the funds I had loaned him. Obviously, this increased my level of financial and emotional stress. But, eventually, because I hounded him like a bill collector he made up for this deficiency through periodic payments when the cottages were doing better.

Odd Jobs

I worked at a variety of part-time jobs during my years at Boston College while I was attending classes full-time days.

At Massachusetts Osteopathic Hospital in Boston near the V.A. Hospital, I served as a part-time custodian, working on weekends and holidays. When the full-time workers were elsewhere, I was waxing and buffing floors in patients' rooms and in the corridors. In addition, one of my functions there was to carry surgical leftovers to the incinerator.

The early months of the hospital job coincided with a distressing fatigue that worried me. I was more than just tired; I was utterly exhausted. So I checked into medical texts at the hospital's library to figure out my symptoms.

The best I could find was "neurasthenia." It was described as "an emotional and psychic disorder characterized by easy fatigability and often by lack of motivation, feelings of inadequacy, and psychosomatic symptoms."

I didn't like the words "disorder" and "psychosomatic" but I have had the symptoms of chronic fatigue throughout most of my long life, and despite obvious endurance I have had very little physical stamina except in short bursts.

Instead, I was gifted with brain energy and determination. Ironically, it could be that my excessive use of my brain drained off energy my body needed. After all, both mental and physical energy can deplete reserves.

In another job that drained energy I was a salesman for the Catholic magazine *Extension*. I remember getting an "advance" that helped for a while with this "working my way through college" job but commissions I earned had to be applied toward the advance. As I've noted before, I was not a very effective salesman. Therefore, the job did not last long.

However, I clearly recall the kindness of *Extension's* area supervisor whose name was Josef Harajovic. I was on a starvation diet at Granny's house at the time. When he invited me to dine with him and his family of immigrants it was like a sample of Paradise. Delicious food was served in a fine house with gracious people. It was a taste of family life that was quite foreign to me.

Obviously, when food and work coincided, that pleased me very much. One such job was short order cook at a Howard Johnson's restaurant. There was a time when one could easily find a Howard Johnson's (HoJo's) on any major highway. In Dedham it was found on Route One near Route 128. When the original restaurant burned down in the '40s it was replaced by a temporary structure resembling a diner.

Dave Rothwell, who had been my close friend at Mrs. White's, was living in the Hyde Park section of Boston and joined me to work at the Dedham HoJo's. We were stationed behind one very long counter where we offered a variety of ice cream dishes, fries, and a limited short order menu. Hamburgers, hot dogs, fried clam strips, and grilled cheese sandwiches were the most popular.

We would take turns at the grill. For a burger we would use an ice cream scoop and smooth the raw ground beef into the scoop, plop it onto the counter, then press it down flat with the palms of our bare hands, and fry it on the grill.

Since the patty contained so much fat, by the time we had cooked it there was almost nothing left but overcooked meat the size of a fifty-cent piece. We would put the burger in a buttered toasted roll and hide the meat by smothering it with relish and whatever else the customer requested. The more filler the better. Actually, the "burger" was just an illusion.

The hot dogs were another matter. The refrigerator was ancient and didn't do a very good job of keeping its contents cold. So the hot dogs tended to have a gray coating on them which we would have to wash off before frying on the greasy grill. Since that time I have had a trust issue when it comes to hot dogs being fresh and edible.

At Christmas time there was usually work in the Dedham Post Office where my father had once risen to the post of Superintendent of Mails and later demoted himself because of other priorities such as planning to resign from the job.

Sometimes at the Christmas season I also worked at the massive South Postal Annex in Boston near South Station. I will never forget the huge boxlike tunnels suspended from the high ceiling so inspectors could look down through peep holes to make sure nobody down below was stealing.

In Dedham the process of sorting was very orderly but in the mammoth Boston facility the only words I can use to describe it are "chaos" and "confusion."

People didn't seem to know who they were working for. "Supervisor? What supervisor?" I am surprised that any of the mail reached its intended destination. But apparently only a small percentage ended up in the Dead Letter Office.

Building Houses

For a couple of summers during college my pals and I worked for a small contractor, Carl Watt, who built houses "on spec," meaning speculation. He also built some homes to a customer's order. He concentrated on the suburbs west of Boston where I worked on houses and small apartment buildings in Needham, Waltham, Newton and Medfield.

The contractor used to call the four of us Jim no matter what our name might be, so after a while we called each other Jim and even called him Jim too. Everybody on each job was Jim! "Hey Jim, give me a hand over here!"

Oh yes, Watt had a supervisor for us named Earl, a very serious man, and we didn't call him Jim. He was Earl and had the status of "foreman." He was a "finish carpenter" and we were "carpenter's helpers." But we served as full fledged carpenters, at much lower pay, doing all the work on a house that was considered "rough" carpentry while saving the finish carpentry for the more highly skilled craftsmen.

I was in my late teens at this time, in the early 1950s, and there were many military veterans on Carl Watt's projects. They were rugged, hard working, heavy drinking guys who drank beer on the job, especially when they were celebrating completion of some portion of the house. The big drinking event was when the roof was framed in and shingled.

On one occasion I found myself as the only helper working with a seasoned carpenter. We did a lot of beer drinking and worked hard as we framed in a whole house. I am still amazed as I reflect back on how the two of us, with him in the lead, framed a house from the foundation to the top of the roof in seven days. This included shingling the roof and installing the windows.

It showed me what a couple of people working together could accomplish. The man I worked with was highly skilled and knew exactly what steps to take to reach his construction goals. And that certainly made all the difference.

On a typical day of work with Watt's regular crew, I joined the older men at lunch but didn't have the alcohol consumption capacity they had. Since they also drank after work before going home, I was part of that process too and I recall too many times when I could hardly see the painted lines on the roads during my return trip to Granny's house in Dedham. I was lucky to survive those experiences.

I was also fortunate to avoid many accidents which accompany the hazardous way of life on construction sites. It was common for workers to fall from a ladder or fall through temporary steps and end up straddling a riser.

Once in a while it was my turn to have a mishap. One time I was using a hatchet and tapping it with a hammer to trim the edge of a "rake" which is a board that runs along the slope of a roof.

One tap by my hammer dislodged a small piece of steel from the hatchet and it came flying at my head like shrapnel, entering my forehead. It bled for a while and I saw a doctor about it but I don't believe it was ever found. We didn't wear protective equipment in those days so I was lucky the piece of metal hadn't hit my unprotected eyes.

Another event I will not forget is when we had asked our boss to hire a college friend of ours who had never worked on construction. The house in Needham near Route 128 was almost roughed in, with the roof on and windows in place when our friend was asked to go to the cellar and get 2 by 4s.

Before the concrete and steel columns are installed in a cellar, temporary "X frames" made of 2 by 4s are used to support the house. Our friend had chosen one of these supports as the source of the 2 by 4s he was going to fetch.

He hammered an X frame with a sledge to knock it out of position, and moments later the whole house began to creak and sink. Then he came running upstairs yelling, "The house is doing a Spanish fandango down there!"

The house was soon jacked up to its approximate position

prior to our friend's mistake, but every nail in the house had been loosened. So we were all on our knees for quite some time pounding on the loose nails.

Obviously, the loosened nails under the roof shingles couldn't be dealt with because we would have had to remove every shingle. So, to this day, every time I drive by that area on Route 128 I still wonder how that home's shingles held up. Not to mention the rest of the house.

My friend was dismissed from that job without delay. I'm sure he learned a lesson or two that day. I also learned many lessons working on construction.

One lesson taught me that the best carpenters were those who knew how to correct their mistakes effectively. I have been able to apply that guideline to every job I have ever held. Admitting a mistake and knowing how to correct it is an important factor in the pursuit of success.

Another lesson learned while building houses was not to strain while using a hand saw. A veteran carpenter was watching my saw buckle each time I tried to saw a piece of wet green lumber. He said, "Just let the saw do the cutting, Tom. Don't try to force it." Forcing it made the saw bind but letting the saw do the cutting worked just fine. This lesson has also followed me through life. The slogan "Easy Does It" helps a lot during times of stress or adversity.

Factories and Landscaping

Filling in gaps in employment, I experienced a number of brief factory jobs. For a while I worked at a woolen mill in Canton that produced wide conveyor belts. The loud clatter of the machinery was a sensation that penetrated my bones.

I only worked there a few months but while there I recall trying to convert one of the workers into a college student. I explained to the World War II vet how he could use his G.I. Bill of Rights to finance a higher education. I encouraged him to improve himself, but he said, "I'm doing fine right where I am." He was not impressed by my suggestion.

One of my unusual short-term jobs was at a cotton waste recycling plant, also in Canton. I was allergic to the whole environment. There were clouds of tiny cotton particles in the air that irritated my eyes and my sinuses, and who knows what effect they had on my lungs?

My job was to run a baling machine into which I poured baskets of shredded cotton. I was told that the product would eventually be used as guncotton. After pouring the cotton into the baler I would operate the machine.

The baler was several feet high and shaped like a huge box standing on its end. When I pressed a button a steel plate would descend and scrunch the loose cotton into a tighter compressed mass that eventually would provide a bale. Then I would add the steel baling strips and tighten them, hoping the flat bands wouldn't break and come flying at me.

Most of the time I was successful at this job. But no matter how much eye solution I used, nothing helped reduce the constant irritation. "Tote that barge, lift that bale…"

Most of the employees there were recent immigrants. So I tried to tell those who could understand English that they didn't have to work in an unhealthy setting. They were not interested in my ideas. Maybe they were what we called "illegal aliens," today's "undocumented immigrants."

Somebody must have told management about my advice because when they closed for a summer vacation I was told, "You don't need to come back after the shutdown." Maybe they figured I was trying to get a union started.

Soon I found work in a plastics factory on Route One in Norwood. The job ended almost as fast as it had begun. I was supposed to stand at a huge circular saw that had no guards and then cut long tubes of plastic into shorter pieces.

Although I had goggles to protect my eyes from flying plastic shards, I was otherwise unprotected. I decided that it was important to my future to keep my fingers and other body parts intact. Therefore, when it came time for lunch I simply walked away and never returned to ask for my pay for the four hours.

My work with a landscaping company was also quickly over and done with. Not that there was flying plastic coming at me, but I just wasn't built for that kind of manual labor. I spent one hot morning shoveling loam from a huge pile into a wheelbarrow, then dumping and spreading it near the house in an area that would eventually become a lawn.

To me, this task seemed endless. One morning was enough. So I disappeared at lunch time and didn't bother to say goodbye or ask for any pay from that organization. Come to think of it, this quiet method of departure became my way of operating with several short-term jobs that didn't suit me.

These jobs as an unskilled laborer were obtained from the Commonwealth of Massachusetts' employment service and required no experience. Also, there was no need to get a reference from those employers. Therefore, I decided not to clutter up my work record with these work episodes.

In some aspects of life, the less said the better. Why confuse other people who have a radically different viewpoint from mine? Discretion is a necessary part of developing a work history.

Besides, these brief unskilled work episodes would be irrelevant when I finally completed Boston College.

6.
DROPPING OUT OF B.C. & TRANSITION JOBS
You are being led (God Calling)

Transition Jobs

As I approached the junior year at Boston College, I was achieving Dean's List grades but my health was in jeopardy. I was experiencing a cluster of frightening symptoms. Heart palpitations. Pulse racing twice as fast as normal. Dizzy spells. Muscular twitches. General weakness.

It was obvious that I had used up all of my reserve energy and was "running on empty." The family doctor suggested rest but going to college full-time and needing to work to survive, I saw no way to follow his advice. Rest? How?

Also, I'm sure the malnutrition diet I lived on at Granny's house wasn't helping the situation. I can still recall Granny saying, "All I need is a bit of tea and toast." Gandhi could have taken lessons from her. But except for my extremely thin body I was definitely not a Gandhi type.

In my effort to get myself through Boston College, I had continued to maintain high grades and was pushing my luck physically with part-time jobs. And money was always in short supply. For a couple of semesters I received some help from the Father Fleming Scholarship Fund at St. Mary's Parish in Dedham. But when it came to financial survival I was always operating on the anxious edge.

In addition, despite my low income status I figured I owed it to myself to have some exciting times with friends. Even though I had a deficit of energy as well as money, I still followed the old idea that "All work and no play makes Jack a dull boy."

Observing my behavior, my Irish grandmother cautioned, "Sure and ye're burning the candle at both ends." She was not exaggerating. Actually, I had exceeded my own limits.

Then, during my junior year at B.C. I fell in love with Mary Killoren who had also been raised in Norwood. That relationship was high on the priority list, so I soon began to see the possibility of taking some time away from college. And Mary agreed with me about my strategy.

My master plan was to drop out of college after my junior year, volunteer to be drafted into the Army, marry Mary, get our own apartment, serve my two years of military service when called by the Draft Board in Dedham, then return as a military veteran to complete Boston College with the help of the G. I. Bill of Rights. It sounded like a good plan.

In the meantime, there were some transition jobs to experience. In the summer of 1953, shortly after I had completed my junior year at B.C., Mary and I became engaged. At that time I was working as a shipper at Dowding Tap Company in a Norwood industrial park.

An example of a "tap" is the metal that creates the grooved sleeve in an auto engine block where the spark plug is inserted. Dowding fashioned pieces of metal that looked just like drill bits. These were the taps that made the grooves.

In the mail room, I inserted the taps into boxes that were shipped throughout the U.S. and abroad. It was not a difficult job except for the fact that I was not allowed to sit down while working. But standing in one spot drained my energy.

When I began to drag a machinist's high chair to my work station, my supervisor found it unacceptable. He apparently equated real "work" with standing. But I was in such a state of exhaustion I could not stand for long periods of time. So I kept getting myself chairs. It wasn't long before I was terminated, just before our marriage that November.

This was not a good time to be out of work. Then, a few days before the marriage ceremony, I found the job that would take me through the winter and into the spring when I believed the Army would induct me. It was my waiting-to-be-drafted job.

I became the time keeper on a construction site in Dorchester where the College Town Sportswear building was being erected. The location was right next door to the new facilities of the *Boston Globe* on Morrissey Boulevard near Boston Harbor. The *Globe* had moved out from the congested downtown Boston area called "Newspaper Row."

Across the street from us there was a massive high rise public housing structure going up. It was described as Columbia Point, named for its location. It turned out to be a disaster in many ways. For example, the police became wary of entering the buildings because it was very hazardous duty. Also, for similar personal safety reasons, taxi cabs often refused to enter the project to pick up and deliver people.

Eventually, the high rise project, despite the Utopian planning that had created it, had to be abandoned. It was ill conceived like most Utopian ideas. One major error was mixing elderly units with units where wild teens lived and threatened the peace of mind and the physical well being of the senior citizens. Robberies and vandalism abounded.

On my side of the boulevard, my job with the Zoppo construction company was easy. I just had to keep track of the workers' time, hand out their paychecks once a week, call the ambulance when necessary, and answer the phone when the "super," or superintendent, was not in the office.

We were housed in a temporary structure about one notch above a shack. But it was well heated and the super was an easygoing but efficient John Wayne type. It was not his fault that so many accidents happened. Accidents were a way of life on construction sites and in those days accident prevention measures were not very thorough.

At the College Town Sportswear site, I reported a wide variety of accidents. For example, a worker who was two or three stories off the ground might drop something like a hammer that landed on a man working on the first floor. Also, falls from various heights were very common. And cuts were always happening.

While we had our share of accidents on our side of Morrissey Boulevard, across the street the high rise Columbia Point buildings were constantly attracting ambulances. One common accident involved men being blown off buildings by gusts of wind while they were several stories up in the air carrying 4' x 8' sheets of plywood.

If a worker was standing on the wrong side of the plywood, a gust would lift him up like a huge kite. Then he and the wood plunged to the earth from a very high place. As we used to say, "It isn't the fall that hurts; it's the sudden stop." The sudden stops led to very severe injuries.

I had lots of down time on my time keeper job. Luckily, they permitted me to read books. So that winter I sat comfortably reading next to the roaring heater that belched warmth to offset the frigid weather.

As we entered 1954 I read extensively during those winter months, including Russian classics and British mysteries. It was probably the ideal job for a person such as I who shunned physical work and enjoyed reading.

Around this time, Mary was working in Boston near the downtown area at a clerical job and met a woman there who gave her some information that changed my own life. Mary said this woman had made a decision early in life never to stay in one job more than five years. To avoid getting "stale" she had taken many jobs. Because of the variety she was a very interesting person with vast experience.

For me, this information struck a responsive chord so I believe I said to Mary, "That sounds good to me." The story that Mary had passed on to me actually helped me to launch my own series of five-year plans.

Unlike the Russian five-year plans designed to lead to world domination, mine was designed to maintain my individual freedom from the imprisonment of lengthy employment. Actually, there were times when I would not even wait for the five years to expire.

I was twenty-one years old then and for a long time I had been surrounded by older folks who stayed in jobs that promised retirement income. They had experienced the Great

Depression and naturally were terrified of unemployment. Their fear kept them in what I called "work bondage."

Those were the days when many people with an Irish heritage chose work with police and fire departments and other government jobs at local, state and federal levels. Uncle Bill was a public school custodian. Uncle Joe worked for the federal government in a civil service job. And my father worked for the U.S. Postal Service.

The men in my family of origin opted for secure work and a retirement plan. To the contrary, the approach to work that I chose was based on a lack of concern with security and total disinterest in the idea of working toward retirement. Security? Who needs it? Retirement? Forget it. I simply would not retire, that's all. I would keep working.

I certainly wouldn't retire from the U.S. Army, that's for sure. I would work at my construction timekeeper job until the draft took me. Then I would put in my military time, return to Boston College for my senior year, and after graduation I would go off into the sunset on some kind of career path that pleased me.

During my two years as a citizen soldier, who could tell what jobs the military would require me to do? That remained to be seen.

7.
THE U.S. ARMY & MORE TRANSITION JOBS
Trust and be not afraid (God Calling)

The U.S. Army

Since I have written another book about my Army experiences, I am not going to dwell on that part of my life now. I will just make a few work-related comments. If you are interested in my misadventures as a military misfit you may get a copy of *Bugging Out: An Army Memoir* (1954).

In March 1954 when the hostilities in Korea had halted and the Vietnam era was impending, I was drafted into the U.S. Army for two years even though I was married and we were expecting our first child. That status would have been grounds for staying out of the military completely, but my own master plan included voluntary service in the Army.

Obviously, because I planned to be a voluntary draftee, the idea of avoiding the draft had no place in my thinking. So, after my junior year at Boston College, I had notified my Draft Board in Dedham that I had not returned to college and was now available. The rest was military misfit history.

In March 1954 I began to serve my two years as a military misfit, starting as a buck private. Although I was basically unsuited for the military life, I have always had a very strong will and once I made my mind up about something it was very hard for me to get sidetracked.

My plan was to serve in the lowest Army ranks to get the G.I. Bill of Rights which would subsidize my senior year at Boston College. So I doggedly pursued that course of action.

Although I had intelligence test scores in basic training that made me eligible for Officers Candidate School, I rejected that opportunity because of my allergic reaction to the Army way of life. Becoming an officer would have extended my length of service beyond the two years draftees served. I thought two years would be plenty.

On reflection, the Army provided some of the most desperate parts of my emotional life. The Army gave me hints about what it would be like to live in a totalitarian society where individual freedom was forbidden and institutional correctness was the standard for all behavior.

The Army also provided some training that has been very useful throughout my adult life. I learned to touch type while I was with the Army's only Military Government (MG) Group at Camp Gordon, Georgia. Also, I gained some useful experience as feature editor of our MG newspaper.

In the mid 1950s as the MG message center clerk, with my cartridge belt around my waist and my .45 in its holster, I was privy to inside information about the Army's future plan to provide military government to a mythical nation in Southeast Asia that was on an instructional map. It was shaped exactly like what we now describe as Vietnam.

We had learned nothing from the departure of the French from that part of the world. After a terrible loss, the French had pulled out while I was in basic training. Then we had been told in clear English, "Your asses will end up in Indo-China." For me, that did not happen. I was lucky.

Following my service with Military Government, I became a public information writer for The Provost Marshal General's School (PMGS), also at Camp Gordon. This was the Army's higher education institution for Military Police officers who might be destined to become future generals.

Working as a public information specialist for PMGS gave me the opportunity to write many articles published in military and civilian newspapers and magazines. It was excellent experience in journalism that I assumed would help me after my return to civilian life.

More "Transition" Jobs

After being honorably and miraculously discharged from the Army in March 1956 without being court-martialed due to my resistance to arbitrary authority, I was back home in

Massachusetts where there were more "transition" jobs to endure while I waited to start my senior year at Boston College. Some of these jobs were on night shifts while I was attending college full-time days. After all, I was the bread winner for a family of three now.

In my first job after the Army, while Mary and I and little Peggy lived with Mary's folks in Franklin, Massachusetts, my Army experience as a message center clerk helped me to win a job as billing machine operator at Lawson's Express, a trucking company in Ashland, Massachusetts.

At Lawson's I recall making significant errors on address labels that resulted in large shipments of material to places far from their intended destination. Although my skill improved, I didn't stay there more than a few months.

Our family of three soon moved from Mary's parents' home in Franklin to our own third-floor apartment in Norwood. With its sloped ceilings, it was a place that was sweltering hot in the summer and cold in the fall and winter. Little Peggy, who was just learning how to talk, made one memorable comment about the apartment: "Too high."

I had found work in that town at the Plimpton Press which printed Mary Baker Eddy's Christian Science works and many other books. It was not difficult work and the job taught me that night shifts were good because the big shots were gone for the day and the rate of pay was slightly higher.

My work at the press was similar to my functions at the Boston Envelope Company on the day shift years before. This time I supplied book covers to machines that glued and attached covers to text pages. I hauled pallets of the finished books to another location in the factory for shipment.

At Plimpton Press I was working the evening shift from four to midnight during my senior year at Boston College where I had a full-time day schedule. Fortunately, there was down time on the job that permitted me to get some studying done. The fact that the shift ended at midnight made the work bearable. But they had a habit of laying people off around Christmas time. And that's what happened to me.

Around that time we had left the third floor apartment that my daughter said was "too high" and we lived in Dedham's Veterans Housing project in a very suitable row house. Our rent was modest so we managed to make ends meet.

The next factory job became available right after I was discharged from Plimpton Press during the Holidays. That work would last me until I graduated from Boston College.

Without any gap in employment, I became an unskilled machine operator at MacGregor Instrument Company in Needham, Massachusetts, working a shift from five p.m. to eleven. This fit in nicely with my college schedule and it was not a physically strenuous or mentally stressful job.

At MacGregor, they manufactured glass hypodermic syringes. As one of the links in an assembly line, I sat in a fairly high chair like the ones they had refused to let me sit in at Dowding Tap Company.

Also, I wore goggles to deal with tiny flying particles. My job was to insert the tips of hundreds of cylinders of glass, one at a time, against a rapidly moving abrasive belt over which water flowed to cool the process.

This procedure removed the dark brown tip of the glass tube that had been intentionally burned in a previous part of the process. As I inserted the cylinder to grind the tip, despite rubber gloves, the abrasive liquid with its ground glass flowed over the portion of my right hand between index and middle fingers, causing a skin irritation that remained with me long after I left the job several months later.

Between the income from MacGregor Instrument and the allowance from the G.I. Bill we were able to get through my senior year of college. To make the senior year even more interesting, our family of three became a family of four that spring when our second daughter, Karen, was born.

Originally, I had been with the Class of 1954 at B.C., but after my return following Army service I was with the Class of 1957. So I ended up in both yearbooks. As an alumnus I still hang out with the class of '54 because I spent three years with them and made lasting friendships there.

In 1957, when I received the Bachelor of Arts Degree *cum laude* in History and Government from the College of Arts and Sciences at Boston College, I was ranked 22nd in a class of 307 students. I considered this a good showing for the Catholic Charities kid who had lived next to the railroad tracks, on the wrong side, and had not attended any prep school as many of my classmates had done.

While completing my senior year at B.C. I applied at Boston University's Graduate School of Arts and Sciences for entrance into the Master of Arts in History program. I was accepted on a part-time basis.

I felt it was important for me to continue my higher education but not for practical reasons. I simply wanted to broaden my mind. In most of my classes at B.U. my classmates were teachers who willingly admitted that they were going for the Master's to increase their income. I came off as an anomaly of sorts, but that role seems to suit me.

It was helpful that the G.I. Bill was available to me for part-time studies. In those days if a person was attending as a part-timer at B.U. we got only two credits for each course instead of the usual three. Therefore, to amass the necessary thirty credit hours I had to complete fifteen courses instead of ten. But this gave me the opportunity to take some courses I might never have taken, including History of Modern Art.

In 1957, at the time I graduated from Boston College, we were experiencing the recession of 1957-58. However, there were some jobs available. Mr. Donaldson at B.C. had a little office where he posted jobs but most of them were sales positions with organizations such as Procter & Gamble.

As a fundamental introvert I was not a candidate for sales jobs. I was interested in a career in journalism. But where? Mr. Donaldson gave me this guidance: "Decide if you want to leave Massachusetts and go somewhere like New York where you will be a small fish in a large pond. Or stay in this area and become a large fish in a smaller pond."

I decided to stay in Massachusetts. However, after exploring the world of Boston area newspapers, I learned that they rarely had openings for reporters. Also, entry level pay was far less than I needed to support my growing family.

Although I wanted to write for a living I had to face reality and obtain work that fit my situation. In a burst of uncharacteristic practicality, I decided to sign up with Peters' employment agency in Boston because I had heard good reports about their quality and integrity.

Following up some of their leads, I found an occupation that made sense to me at that time in my life.

8.
AUTOMOBILE MUTUAL INSURANCE COMPANY
All is well (God Calling)

Amica Mutual Insurance Company

The Boston office of Automobile Mutual Insurance Company of America (AMICA), with its home office in Providence, Rhode Island, was looking for college graduates to fill positions as claims investigators dealing with auto accidents in the Greater Boston area.

In those days Amica was often called Factory Mutual because Factory Mutual Liability Insurance Company of America (FMLICA) and AMICA operated under the same umbrella. Our pay checks came from both organizations. When we told other insurance people where we were from, we just said "Factory." Eventually, that shifted to "Amica."

Because accident investigation sounded very interesting, I took the interview. Shortly after that I was hired for the Boston Office at a rate of pay substantially higher than the salary I had been earning at MacGregor Instrument Company. Also, a new company car came with the job.

In those days if you had a company car and made about $5,000 a year or $100 a week you felt upwardly mobile. You could afford a house payment or rent of about $100 a month and begin to move into the vast middle class. But first it was necessary to establish a credit status and put in some time at the new occupation to demonstrate your fiscal stability.

My first weeks with Amica were spent familiarizing myself with procedure in the large Boston branch office with its long rows of perfectly aligned desks. The office had a striking resemblance to the office scene depicted in a film with Jack Lemmon titled "The Apartment."

Our office was up a few flights in the Park Square Building in the central city a short walk from Boston Common. Looking out of the office windows high above the street below I could see people marching toward the steps leading down to the mass transit trains, known as "The El" or the MTA, meaning the Metropolitan Transit Authority.

The people down below seemed like ants in a Kafkaesque human ant hill. Because I did not want to spend my life that way, I was grateful that I would only be in and out of the urban ant hill on two or three afternoons a week.

Soon I was assigned to ride for a few weeks with an experienced adjuster in the Greater Boston area, learning the ropes. I shadowed him as a passenger in his company car while he was investigating a variety of claims.

We were called "adjusters" but "Claims Representative"

was the more accurate description on our business cards. The details of figuring out the exact damages to a vehicle and negotiating repair costs were outsourced to professional property damage adjusters attached to body shops such as Cambridge Auto Metal.

Our investigations focused on interviews related to the liability aspects of a case, i.e. who was at fault. After the training weeks, during which I was introduced to the organization's personnel policies, I was given the new Ford Fairlane company car with Amica's special blue color, a shiny leather briefcase, and a camera. This was the first time I had total use of a new automobile, and I was elated.

The organization widely known today as Amica had a dress code then that was fairly strict because the company took great pride in its reputation as an elite insurance carrier. It was a company that specialized in "preferred risks." So its executives were supposed to look the part.

We were required to wear dress suits and ties. No sport shirts and no sport coats were allowed. Also, we had to wear felt hats, not caps, and London Fog raincoats. We wore standard leather shoes, not loafers. Absolutely no sneakers! We were expected to be well groomed at all times while representing Amica. No long hair. Clean shaven.

The new position was quite a transition for me to

experience in June 1957 shortly after graduating from Boston College. The leap from student with a factory job to junior executive with a leading insurance carrier was dramatic and the transition was quick.

On a Friday I was a night shift factory worker at a small plant in Needham and the following Monday I was a young executive representing the Boston office of one of the most highly respected insurance carriers in the U.S.

The new look I presented at the veterans housing project was dramatic too. In close neighborhoods like housing projects everybody notices the visible details pertaining to their neighbors' lives, especially when a new car pulls in behind the row house and the next day the man of the house goes off to work dressed up in a suit, with a briefcase.

There was an abundance of freedom in the work of a claims investigator. I appreciated that. We only had to show up at the Boston office every other afternoon on a rotating schedule. One week it would be Tuesday and Thursday. The following week it would be Monday, Wednesday and Friday.

On the afternoon in the office we would obtain the files for each case we were working on and dictate our reports into a Dictaphone which would then be transcribed in the secretarial pool and returned to us as typed copy.

We would also sit with our claims supervisor who went

over our new cases with us and discussed our progress on existing cases. My supervisor Ray Terrell, a seasoned claims executive, was excellent to work with and eventually became manager of a branch office somewhere else in the Bay State.

As a claims rep I spent most of my time in the field within a territory of Suffolk and Norfolk counties. Suffolk County included the city of Boston. Norfolk County embraced many "blue chip" suburbs west and south of Boston.

Most of my cases were auto accidents and as time went by I investigated some home owners' insurance claims as well. The severity of the auto cases ranged from minor all the way up to seriously injured and fatal.

Once we had been assigned a case, we made our own appointments to interview those we insured, claimants, and witnesses. We took photos of damaged vehicles, and photographed the scene of the accident which was called "the locus," Latin for "place." We visited police stations for accident reports, and sometimes observed cases in courtrooms. It was always interesting work.

As I look back on those years, I compare the work to having almost as much freedom as a cowboy, freely riding the range of city and suburb, arranging my own schedule, and making brief contacts with my supervisor in the Boston office, back at the ranch.

The freedom suited my independent personality. I enjoyed making my own decisions. Maybe that's why the song "Don't Fence Me In" has always been one of my favorites.

The work had a combination of factors that made each day an adventure of sorts. Although folks we insured tended to come from affluent suburbs, those who were involved in accidents with our policyholders could come from just about anywhere within my territory and also in adjacent counties.

In my territory I had city, suburban and country settings. When I had a case involving somebody outside my territory it could be just about anywhere in the Greater Boston area. This gave each day variety.

In the morning I might be visiting a mansion resembling a Greek temple in an affluent suburb such as Weston, Cohasset or Dover. That same afternoon I could be in Dorchester, Roxbury or East Boston, interviewing a driver in an apartment with a defective space heater in a very rundown three-story tenement, i.e. "triple decker."

Also, I saw many people at their jobs in just about every imaginable work situation in government or the private sector. I interviewed politicians at the State House, visited writers at newspapers such as the Boston Globe, the Herald, and Record-American, saw lawyers in their plush State Street offices near the downtown Boston area, and took statements from shipyard workers in Quincy.

Most of my cases involved auto accidents, but as the years passed I investigated a substantial number of home owners' insurance claims. One of them left a vivid memory.

In Norwood near New Pond a very large pheasant had mistaken a picture window for open space because the picture window at the front of the house had been directly in line with a slider at the other end of the home. The bird had flown at high speed right through the window, shattering it, and then it had died in the living room after flailing around on a brand new white rug. It was a colossal bloody mess.

Between the auto accidents and the wide variety of home owners' claims, it is no exaggeration to say that working for Amica was challenging and interesting. I cannot think of many jobs that would expose a person to just about every aspect of modern civilization. Mine was that job.

From time to time in the inner city I would find myself climbing many flights of stairs, knocking on a door, and being answered by a tough customer wearing a green eyeshade, holding his playing cards in his hand, and growling, "What the hell do ya want, pal?"

The attitude changed when I said I might have some money for someone, but otherwise they might not be pleased with my visit. I always felt relieved to leave those places, took a quick photo of the damaged vehicle in the driveway, and made my exit from the neighborhood.

I can still remember the case in which an enraged driver that we insured kept intentionally rear ending the car ahead of him all the way up a steep hill behind the State House. He did extensive damage to the rear of the other car and the front of his own. Obviously, our driver had a serious anger management problem. Or was he mentally ill?

I recall the woman in Milton who hopped into her car in her garage one morning and hit the gas pedal, thinking she was in reverse. Instead, she was in drive. As she pressed down on the gas pedal, she went plowing through the rear wall of her garage, demolished much of that building, and continued to sail across her lawn. She destroyed various shrubs and other objects before coming to rest against her own house with a severely damaged car and extensive damage to her property. Luckily, her injuries were minor.

I also remember the case in Medfield in which a man we insured was driving in bad weather and couldn't stop when a prize Brahma bull suddenly appeared before his eyes. He did fatal damage to the bull and serious damage to his own car. He was lucky to survive the accident.

One memory deeply imprinted in my psyche was the fatal accident in Needham in which a young newly licensed driver had lost control at high speed and wrapped his car around a tree. The shape of the tree was easily seen in the car wreck. And the young man's bloody shoes were still on the floor of the car when I took a picture of it.

Another fatal accident I recall was not one of my cases. A man had pulled over to the side of a highway to make a call from a phone booth. While he was making his call a car passed, towing a boat. The trailer hookup let go and the detached boat demolished both the phone booth and the unlucky man who had decided to use that phone.

During the five years I investigated claims for Amica, I learned much about the relativity of truth. To arrive at some semblance of truth I interviewed drivers, passengers and witnesses as I tried to reach a balanced decision. Up to a certain level I had discretion, and after that I would refer the decision to my supervisor who might involve our legal team.

I had learned early in the game as a claims investigator that when it comes to money matters many people think lying is trivial. So they do it without guilt.

An example of outright lying was a case in which the person we insured was rear-ended when she stopped for a red light in the Hyde Park section of Boston. The driver who caused the damage later claimed that the car ahead had backed up into his car. There were witnesses that attested to the truth. So, obviously, we refused to pay the claimant.

All in all, my years with Amica were positive ones. I made many good friends there. With steady pay raises, Mary and I soon became able to afford to build our first house in the suburb of Franklin. It was a fairly roomy Cape Cod style home, with a large breezeway and garage attached, on a sizable lot at the end of a dead-end street that provided much privacy and a safe location for our family of four.

In 1961, the year my third daughter Amy was born, we became a family of five and I had also achieved my educational goal. After my four years of graduate study in U.S. and European History at Boston University's Graduate School of Arts and Sciences, I was awarded the Master of Arts degree in History.

I had been the first in my family of origin to graduate from college and now I was first to achieve a Master's Degree. It felt good. But I was not competing with anybody, just pursuing my own personal development.

By this time my five-year plan was moving steadily toward decision time. At Amica in those days when a claims rep had five or six years of experience under his belt, and an excellent work record, he was in position for promotion to the role of claims supervisor either in the Boston office, one of Amica's branches, or the Home Office in Providence, R.I.

One problem with promotion to supervisor was that the move from field work to inside office work required turning in the company car. This meant I would have to replace the car with my own vehicle, and that major expense was like a reduction in pay, even though there was a good raise that would accompany the promotion.

Even more of a problem for me was the transition from great freedom of movement to sitting at a desk five days a week as one of the claims supervisors. I simply could not picture doing that.

During my years with the rotating schedule of every other afternoon in the office I usually ended up with a headache before it was time to leave the office and drive out of the city. So, for me the idea of choosing to endure daily office work seemed like a choice for ongoing headaches.

Another important factor was that I was not interested in spending the rest of my work life in the insurance industry. I still had in mind the idea of eventually moving into some kind of employment that included writing. So a turning point had been reached.

In 1962, near the end of the fifth year of my five-year plan, we moved back to Dedham from Franklin to be closer to Boston. Then I began my search for new employment.

9.
PUBLIC INFORMATION AT SAFETY COUNCIL
Desire brings fulfillment (God Calling)

Massachusetts Safety Council Staff

Deciding to do some research into nonprofit public service organizations, I found myself attracted to the mission of the Massachusetts Safety Council, Inc., a private nonprofit accident prevention organization located in Boston.

Having investigated accidents for five years, I figured my experience might appeal to the folks at the Safety Council. So I sent a query letter. Soon afterward, Executive Vice President Bruce Campbell's office called me and arranged to have me come in for an interview.

I did well in the interview with Bruce and another staff executive. Pending approval by the Council's Executive Committee, they offered to make me a staff member in a new position titled Executive Assistant for Fund Raising.

I would coordinate a fund raising effort and when we achieved our fund raising goal, the Council would open up another new position for me that involved extensive writing.

My shift from claims investigator to Executive Assistant at a nonprofit organization was definitely an exercise in downward mobility. The salary was substantially less and I lost the benefit of a company car.

Not only did this mean that I needed to buy a car; I would also have commuting expenses from Dedham to the inner city as I traveled by train. But it was a trade-off I was willing to make. After all, I was moving toward a position that involved writing, my first love. As for the headaches of working a nine-to-five job five days a week, I entered a state of denial about that.

When I became a staff executive at the Safety Council with offices at 54 Devonshire Street in downtown Boston, I acquired a private office, a status symbol of sorts. The windows and window sills collected soot from ancient coal fired heating systems, but it was still a private office.

Across the way in another office building I recall seeing a middle-aged gentleman in a private office who wore a vest and did nothing but read newspapers. His solitary image could have been the subject of an Edward Hopper painting.

Another factor at my new job was that I was accustomed to leaving an office at the end of the day with a totally clean desktop. But at the Council the staff left lots of clutter on top of their desks which made them appear very busy.

From my afternoons in the office at Amica I knew about the unspoken rules of office life. One of them was the need to be busy. At Amica that was done by action, and no clutter.

To avoid being misinterpreted in my work at the Safety Council, I began using desk organizers which I filled with manila file folders. That way, I wasn't lost in clutter but at the same time I looked as busy as I really was.

The goal set for me was to raise the equivalent of my salary that first year. Then my duties would still include coordinating fund raising activities but the bulk of my time would be spent on public information. That was fine by me.

Fund raising, naturally, was about organizing contacts with influential leaders in Massachusetts who would plead our case to their peers. Our Board of Governors was like a *Who's Who* of business, industry and government. So we would use the people on our board to contact their friends and associates at the leadership level in other organizations.

We set up a committee to spark the campaign and they were very effective. I coordinated the communications aspects of the effort through writing newsletters, arranging key appointments, developing solicitation packets, and writing fund raising letters for our people to send as they moved toward a follow-up interview. I also did research through Boston's Kirstein Library where information could be obtained about Boston's corporate and business elite.

The personalized approach is what won the day. As the

coordinator of the fund raising effort I helped achieve the goal of attracting enough new income that year to secure my salary for the following year. This ensured my movement to the post of Public Information Director which fit in nicely with my career goals.

As Public Information Director for the Massachusetts Safety Council, I felt I was in my element as I worked to expand the Council's mass media communication. That was when I had my first experience of being a featured guest on one of Boston's late night radio talk shows.

The host was radio veteran Mike Ehrlich. One of my first lessons from him was the problem of "dead air." He asked me a question and I nodded. But nods can't be seen on radio. So I learned fast, spoke replies instead of using pantomime, avoided dead air, and tried to balance my responses with my host's commentary and callers' comments.

Obviously, the subject that night was highway safety and I was the expert despite my fairly brief experience with the Mass. Safety Council. However, my years of investigating highway accidents for Amica became very useful. Plenty of listeners called in, and as my anxiety decreased I had many excellent chats with callers.

The host explained to me before we went on the air that the length of my presence as a guest on the show would be based on the number of callers. Fortunately, there are many radio listeners late at night from all walks of life. Their calls continued into the wee hours without letup.

That started my love affair with radio, a medium that became very familiar to me as the years passed. Radio people are usually more relaxed, casual in their attire, and more informal than their counterparts on TV.

This part of my life was a time of practical on-the-job education. At the Council, under CEO Bruce Campbell's tutelage I had the opportunity to learn new skills and at the same time overcame my paralyzing fear of public speaking.

In addition to radio appearances, I began to give lectures on highway safety. Sometimes I served as a legislative spokesman at the State House. In this role, I made some presentations at hearings during our campaign to win enactment of a bill requiring compulsory seat belt installation in all new cars sold in Massachusetts.

Through the Council's persistence, the bill eventually passed. When enough states did the same thing, seat belts became standard equipment in automobiles throughout the nation. This was the kind of public service outcome that made my downward mobility feel worthwhile.

While at the Council, I was named to the Sub-Committee on Education of the Governor's Highway Safety Committee, under Governors Endicott Peabody and John Volpe. I met many leaders in government as well as the private sector.

At the annual Massachusetts Safety Conference we had a special Governor's Highway Safety Luncheon with the current Governor providing the keynote address. I recall escorting Governors to the podium. At another function I met newsman Walter Cronkite at the hotel entrance and guided him to the Grand Ballroom for his talk.

Also, I was able to hone my writing skills by producing newsletters about the Council's activities. And I wrote radio and TV public service announcements as well as feature stories for publications such as *Industry* magazine,

Although my work at the Council held my interest, at home I was feeling financial pressure. With mounting fiscal stress, I could not imagine sticking to my five-year employment plan.

The conservative pay structure at the Council was not likely to change and I was becoming ambitious to take on responsibilities higher than staff functions. I wanted to move upward to a leadership role in a nonprofit organization.

Quest for New Employment

In 1964 I began my quest for new employment. One opportunity that seemed to be a natural progression for me was an opening with the City of Boston where they were seeking a coordinator for a new pedestrian safety education program that was soon to be launched.

I waged an intensive personal campaign for the position, using many of the high level contacts I had met during my years fund raising for the Council. They wrote very favorable letters to Mayor John Collins.

The letters were so effective that I received a call from the Mayor's office indicating that enough was enough and they would be in touch with me soon. In other words, it looked as if I might be first in line for the job.

However, at that time I was a finalist for the position of Executive Vice President of The Chevrolet Dealers Association, Inc., representing dealers in Massachusetts and Rhode Island. So I had to make a decision. With the Chevy dealers there would be a higher salary as CEO plus a company car and I wouldn't have to commute to the city.

Although the public service aspects of my work at the Safety Council had suited my personality, for my expanding family the downward mobility had been an ongoing problem.

Now there was the possibility of achieving a Chief Executive post as an association manager, with increased income and the security of a car that was more reliable than my rust bucket Nash Rambler. I chose the Chevy Dealers.

10.

CEO: CHEVROLET DEALERS ASSOCIATION

Trust and pray (God Calling)

The Chevrolet Dealers Association

After competing with about 100 other applicants for the position of Executive Vice President of The Chevrolet Dealers Association, Inc., I won the CEO slot and decided in favor of that job. Among other factors, I opted for the Chevy Dealers job because it required no political "pull."

I preferred to accept the position that was based solely on my own experience and talent. In other words, I favored advancement based on my own merit. My attitude about merit has remained constant through the years, whether applied to myself or others. I believe in the following concise statement: "Equal opportunity based on merit."

A word about job titles here. At the head of most organizations, including charitable groups and trade associations, there is usually a person who is hired by the board of directors to be Chief Executive Officer (CEO).

The title may be President, Executive Vice President, or Executive Director. The job is the same regardless of the title. It's the top executive job and reports to the Board of

Directors. Actually, in conversations I got in the habit of calling myself an Executive Director no matter what my official title was. It was a common title in nonprofits and it seemed easier for people to understand.

I recall how I had mixed feelings on that first day of my new job. I had won the job but I felt a bit confused. Maybe I should say that it felt "odd" for me to be in charge of somebody else's organization. It was to be the first of four experiences in which I was the top executive.

With my independent lone wolf spirit, it had never been easy for me to serve under somebody else's authority. And I certainly desired to be the boss, not a subordinate. But they are not exaggerating when they say, "It's lonely at the top."

Also, there could be some truth in Granny O'Connell's Irish wisdom: "The closer you are to the top the closer you are to the door." I don't know where she got that insight.

Actually, on reflection, in my career as an association executive I was serving as a paid mercenary. After all, I was not a Chevrolet Dealer. And the dealers were people with whom I had very little in common. Yet suddenly I was playing an important role in their ongoing drama of chasing success in the automotive field.

Alone in my Watertown office, I was sitting behind a large oak desk browsing through files and wondering what my first activities might be. The office tucked into one end of the co-op enterprise's warehouse was small and my only secretarial person, a part-timer, was away from the office.

As far as I know, there is no effective training program for one's first job as a parent. The same is usually true with preparation for one's role as a Chief Executive. Three years of very close proximity to our leader Bruce Campbell at the Safety Council was helpful. But each leadership experience is unique regardless of similarities.

At first glance, it seemed that running the Chevrolet Dealers Association might be an uncomplicated job for me. Also, a committee representing the Board of Directors was going to meet with me shortly to go over priorities.

As with all new events in my life, I was anxious as I tried to project a picture of my future with the Chevy Dealers. Yet I knew the situation would soon clarify itself.

A trade association is a different breed of cats from a Safety Council. The Council was a nonprofit charitable organization. The Chevrolet Dealers Association was a trade association that also operated in a nonprofit manner.

Operationally, the two organizations had some structural similarities such as a voluntary Board of Directors and a paid staff. And there were committees to work on various projects determined by the Board. The President of the Board in both cases was a volunteer with flexibility about his leadership style and his relationship with the Chief Executive.

When the directors held the meeting to vote on my acceptance I assumed that the vote would be unanimous in my favor. "All those in favor?" "Aye." It sounded like the whole group had responded in the affirmative.

"All those opposed?" When the query came for the "No" vote, a loud voice boomed out an emphatic "No!" I squirmed in my seat. But this was organizational democracy, with dissent permitted and the majority vote carrying the day. Since I was accepted by the majority, wasn't that enough? Not necessarily.

It turned out that the dissenting board member was angry about the previous CEO being dismissed. So now he was showing his frustration with the majority opinion of his colleagues. And I would soon give him a specific reason to be even more upset with me.

As I reviewed the financial statements of the organization, I learned that he and my predecessor had been close pals and had shared many a fine dinner together at the expense of the association with top shelf alcohol lubricating them at an upscale Italian restaurant in Boston's North End.

He was not enthralled with the report I provided on that relationship to my Board of Directors. As a result, during the years that followed, that dealer turned out to be a constant irritant. Periodically, he used me as the bull's-eye for verbal darts he would throw in my direction.

This brought the beginning of a personal philosophy that I carried with me through the rest of my work life involving groups of people. The philosophy is summed up in the following words: "When you have a picnic it's wise to expect an ant to show up, or even a mosquito."

Right from the outset in my new position, I faced differing opinions on various issues from members of the Board. But I had already learned at the Safety Council that in any committee when a vote is needed one can expect at least three groups of participants in the democratic process.

First, there are the opinion leaders who tend to prevail. Also, there are the chronic dissenters who are compulsively negative. And there are the indecisive middle-of-the-roaders who often play the role of fence sitters and tend to sway with the prevailing winds.

The Chief Executive is involved in an intricate dance with all three groups. For the sake of survival, the CEO must be a diplomat who can create as much harmony as possible.

Working closely with Association President Bob Feely, owner of Feely Chevrolet in Needham, one of my first challenges was the need to move the office to a more convenient location.

The office I inherited in Watertown, a very congested Boston suburb, was attached to an enterprise of the Chevy dealers. The enterprise was a purchasing cooperative through which the dealers would buy auto parts and supplies in bulk and later make substantial profits by selling those items at the dealership level.

Because the association desired to separate itself from the co-op, I was authorized to locate the new office. After surveying key members, I found an excellent spot in the Boston suburb of Braintree.

That town in Boston's South Shore was adjacent to busy highways including the Southeast Expressway, Route 3 and Route 128. These roads provided easy access to Boston and convenient access from every direction for those wishing to visit headquarters.

Relocating the Association's Headquarters

The location I selected was 182 Forbes Road in Braintree in a relatively new office park on Route 128 near the South Shore Plaza. This was just a few miles from my home in the Boston suburb of Dedham, a much easier commute than the Watertown location and its high density traffic.

The first office space I chose had no windows but soon I

shifted to a neighboring office that had very large windows. I had found that the absence of daylight affected my moods, increasing my sense of isolation. Yes, even though I was a lone wolf by nature, one must seek a healthy balance between the social and the solitary, darkness and light.

Starting with one part-time office worker I was soon authorized to expand the office by hiring a full-time secretary, a new experience for me. At Amica we had used a typing/clerical pool and at the Safety Council two or three staff members shared the same secretary.

The main function of the Chevrolet Dealers Association was to arrange board and committee meetings and coordinate educational programs and seminars for the members. In addition, I had to put energy into expanding the membership of the voluntary association.

Membership expansion was a key reason why I was given the company car, a 1964 Chevy Impala convertible. In my daily functioning it was up to me to plan how much time I would give to office work or work out in the field. This was a motivation problem at times because sales activity did not give me much satisfaction. But it had to be done.

Now, with a new car and a higher salary, the challenge of supporting my family was eased. The dealers treated me well. And I enjoyed having my own office arrangement where I was the boss of a small staff and had a long conference table extending out from my massive desk.

We could hold small committee meetings there. But it turned out that the dealers preferred to meet in rooms attached to hotels. When I arranged those rooms for the large membership meetings and the Board of Directors, I would also reserve a room for the card game that a few of the dealers enjoyed after each business meeting.

Preparing for their card game was not an official part of my job description but I was expected to do it. The dealers who gambled played for high stakes, sometimes new cars. For their card game, I had to make sure the hotel provided a private room with a suitable table and a green table cloth. Also, I delivered playing cards that were in their original sealed wrappings.

Some dealers took trips to Las Vegas paid for by the casinos that appreciated their business. When I was asked if I would like to tag along, my reply was simply, "No, thanks." As tempting as the all-expense paid trips were, I was in no position to take financial risks. I had a gambling aspect to my personality, but casino games of chance were not for me.

While I was working with the dealers I learned much about the world of franchising and the inner workings of the automotive industry. General Motors and its Chevrolet

Division were called "the factory" by the dealers. The factory provided franchises that were not guaranteed for life.

The dealers had to function in politically correct ways to please the factory. If the factory was pushing a group advertising concept the dealers needed to sign up, pay their share, and participate enthusiastically. They also had to buy display banners and other gimmicks to enhance sales.

When they were expanding or upgrading their buildings, GM provided advice they needed to accept. When I was with the dealers, GM was in an expansion mood and Detroit put pressure on local dealers to modernize and expand facilities.

Some of the dealers who had paid off their mortgages years before described this process as "building a monument to General Motors." I knew of one case on the North Shore of Massachusetts in which the pressure was so intense that it was rumored to be a factor leading to the dealer's suicide.

Others tried to keep their older facilities for much longer than the factory wished. If you refused to upgrade, very soon you might see a brand new facility a mile or so up the street capturing the customers that used to be yours. This would teach you a lesson about what happened if you bucked the factory's wishes.

Also, if you wanted to keep the dealership in the family and pass the franchise on to your child some day it was not wise to antagonize the factory. The factory had more power over the dealers than the average person knew about.

Through its "Zone office" in Canton near the Route 128 Railroad Station the factory allocated new car shipments to the dealers in the large region. So it was a very good idea to stay on the right side of the Zone Manager.

For example, the Zone Manager was always treated very well at our association functions. When I arranged our annual meeting and outing at Blue Hill Country Club it was important to make sure he won one of the best raffle prizes.

Originally, in the heyday of Chevy sales, the association had engaged primarily in group advertising as a cooperative effort. When Chevrolet was the leader in U.S. car sales, the association took in lots of money and spent vast sums on lavish ad campaigns and group functions.

For example, as part of the celebration party for the new models they might have a full-size copy of the latest model carved in ice. However, when I began serving the association lavish spending was a thing of the past. The membership had experienced drastic shrinkage. Also, I had inherited a deficit.

As I attracted new members, the deficit was gradually eliminated. That put our organization on a sound financial footing. But it was not easy to keep the group's finances in balance. In my capacity as CEO of the Chevrolet Dealers

Association I had to pay close attention to the annual budget because, among other things, my salary was a key factor.

During the first year alone I brought a fifty percent increase in membership while increasing services and lowering dues. It was a very good year and the dealers treated me well with a large raise in pay. It was a far cry from the modest pay at the Safety Council.

Refining My Management Style

However, I had not yet refined my management style when it came to being a CEO. I tended to achieve too much in the early months of my tenure. It would have been wiser to hold a tighter rein on my own zeal in the opening months so my lower intensity wouldn't be obvious when I inevitably began to plateau. "What have you done for us lately, Tom?"

But I had a lot to offer and continued to provide it regularly. My public information experience at the Safety Council came in very handy as I stepped up communication with members through special bulletins, newsletters, and personal contact. Also, I achieved coverage of the group's activities in both state and national media, including specialized nationwide publications like *Automotive News*.

To enhance the educational aspects of the organization, I coordinated seminars, meetings, and conferences. I initiated area meetings to increase member attendance and involvement. And I devised complaint procedures so members could air their grievances.

Also, I developed surveys, polls, and a legislative contact program to back up the political efforts of the statewide auto dealers association.

An important part of my job was attracting experts to provide stimulating lectures that would enhance the dealers' business acumen. I still clearly recall a seminar in which we had an expert in success motivation as our presenter. I remember his advice "not to try to force a market."

Naturally, there are times during the year such as the period right after Christmas when people are not in the mood for large purchases. Advertising money invested during such periods brings little or no return. But if the factory demanded a cooperative advertising campaign in one of these periods, the dealers had to swallow hard and go along with it.

Another piece of advice to the dealers in their role as employers was to keep in mind that salespersons have a mental built-in monthly guide that indicates when they have made enough sales to satisfy their own needs. When they reach that level they put the brakes on their sales energy.

Therefore, since personality plays a great role in the sales process, the presenter stressed to our dealers the importance of screening new applicants for sales jobs carefully with these factors in mind.

I remember another fast talking "expert" who advised the dealers to "sell the sizzle, not the steak." This approach annoyed me, but it is often used in the world of consumer sales and advertising. I find it devious and misleading.

Also, I recall a man visiting my office in Braintree peddling a success motivation course for the dealers to use with their employees. I listened to his pitch and followed him to the exit to observe what kind of a car he drove.

This was my test to see if he practiced what he preached. As I suspected, he owned a decrepit old car. He could talk the talk but he wasn't walking the walk. So I did not encourage my Board of Directors to invite him to present his package for their consideration.

I should mention that there were fringe benefits that came with my job. One of them was a special invitation to a lavish preview of the annual Auto Show at Prudential Center in Boston. It was an impressive production with all the glitz and glamour of a Las Vegas show.

In the lobby of the Prudential Tower as one entered the show, there were three freely flowing alcohol fountains. These were large fountains and next to the fountains were many drinking glasses. One fountain contained Manhattans, another provided Martinis, and the third offered Champagne. Although I was a Scotch drinker, I sampled so much of each fountain that later my friends had to help me to a taxi and then to China Town where I became woozy and ended up sitting near a small decorative waterfall on the steps leading up to the restaurant. At that time, I still had not graduated from booze to plain water and a sober way of life.

On one hand, there was much that was good about my years with the Chevy Dealers. On the other hand, life with the auto dealers was no picnic. These were highly motivated entrepreneurs. Many had inflated egos. And I had to be on high alert with some of them to protect my own sense of self.

One extremely wealthy dealer who wore a special fur coat from the Andes was always trying to get me to wait on him. He would hand me his coat on arrival at a meeting and expect me to keep an eye on it for him. So I learned to say, "I'll find somebody to take care of it for you."

Another dealer would ask me to get him cigars and I would tell him, "I'll find a waiter to run your errand." On one occasion when our evening meeting was over and I was getting on a hotel elevator to head for home, that dealer came rushing after me. As he shouted his request at me, the elevator door began to close so I called out, "Good night," and waved at him with a grin as the door closed completely.

These men were used to being waited on and having their way with subordinates. But this did not fit my independent personality or my role as Executive Director. So I tried to hold onto my own dignity whenever they attempted to take advantage of their presence on my Board of Directors.

One special mosquito at my picnic was nationally known for his expertise in an important segment of the auto industry. He was always trying to sidestep the board and convince me to do favors for him that went very far beyond the boundaries of my job.

Developing a strategy of dealing with him in writing, I took notes on his phone calls and requests, summarized them, kept him at arm's length, and sent copies of my memos to key people in the association with a copy to him as well. This was part of the strategy known as "covering your own ass" which is so necessary in the field of leadership.

Another memorable event in my career with the Chevy Dealers was a discussion with a dealer I had persuaded to join the association. He had become very active and rose to a leadership position. Then he confronted me one day and said, "Tommy, you're a nice guy but I don't think your job should exist. We don't really need a full-time Executive Director."

I don't recall how I responded. It was probably with a remark such as "You're entitled to your opinion." Maybe he had a point, but it was important for me to keep the job going. I had a wife and three daughters to support, and a house to maintain. I had to watch my back, you might say.

Another memory that comes to me periodically is about a very patient gentleman who was an advertising executive with the *Boston Globe*. Bud Owen would often visit me in Braintree. If he arrived shortly after a Board of Directors meeting he unwittingly served as my mental health therapist.

Sitting at board meetings facing a group of unrestrained egotists tested my patience. So I would relate to Bud about the dealers' antics and my reactions. When he left our chat his shoulders would be sinking a bit lower on his torso.

I still feel embarrassed remembering how I unloaded on this gentleman who was so patient. Now I know I could have used a professional psychotherapist during my years as a Chief Executive to help me maintain my mental balance.

Interpersonal relations are never easy when one is working with people who tend toward narcissism. So challenges are unavoidable. The trick is to keep one's own emotional balance as much as possible.

Sometimes I was good at that. Other times I was not. But that's life, right? Also, isn't there more to life than success at work? How about creativity of a higher order?

11.
WRITING & POLITICS & MAINE COAST
In all things seek simplicity (God Calling)

Moving Onward and Upward

During my time with the dealers, I was also giving energy to my own creative writing in the form of novels and essays based on my experiences in life. This activity certainly became my passion. Perhaps I should say my creative writing was addictive.

My writing obsession had all the earmarks of an addiction. I certainly was captured by it, especially when I was writing fiction that was far more challenging and satisfying than the prose I was creating at work.

On the professional front, I joined the New England Society of Association Executives, and eventually served as a member of the organization's Board of Directors. In addition, I was a member of the Publicity Club of Boston.

Also, I tried to fulfill a political craving. While at Boston College a friend had talked me into running for Student Council. I printed a card telling people not to vote for me "…unless you want good government." As I had suggested, they decided not to vote for me. I was soundly defeated.

But the itch to run for elective office remained in my psyche. Eventually, I ran for a seat on the Dedham School Committee, and once again I was soundly defeated.

Then the town moderator appointed me to the Committee to Study Future School Building Needs of the Town of Dedham. Next I became secretary and public information liaison for the group, with high visibility in the local media.

By waging a continuous public information effort, I helped pave the way for community acceptance of a two million dollar high school addition. Also, I wrote an informative brochure for the Town Meeting that approved the bond issue without a dissenting vote.

When I ran for School Committee again the next year, I was elected and then served as member, Vice-Chairman, and in my third year I was elected by my colleagues to be Chairman. At age 34, I was characterized in the local paper, the *Dedham Transcript*, as the youngest School Committee Chairman in the history of the Town of Dedham.

Obviously, I was proud of my upward mobility. The Catholic Charities kid from a group home in Norwood who had later lived with Granny O'Connell next to the East Dedham railroad station on the wrong side of the tracks had climbed another rung higher on my ladder of self-esteem.

There was much satisfaction that came my way during my

years on the School Committee, presiding at meetings, addressing the high school graduating class, and officiating at various functions. Also, I was becoming less introverted during the process. So this was good training for me.

Not only was I serving as Chief Executive of The Chevrolet Dealers Association, I was also overseeing the Dedham school system's annual budget of $3,000,000. I was intimately involved with providing an excellent education for 5,000 public school students and employment of a workforce with more than 300 personnel. I had a full plate.

Among other activities, I helped improve communication between the school system and the public by initiating a newsletter that was circulated several times yearly to taxpayers. Another major achievement was negotiating one of the first collective bargaining contracts for teachers to be agreed upon in Massachusetts.

In addition to stimulating high school expansion, I also pushed for junior high renovation. Another interesting challenge during my tenure as Chairman of the School Committee was the retirement of the Superintendent of Schools and the hiring of a new Chief Executive, Jim Dunne, who was one of the finest gentlemen I had ever known.

Also, I played a role in increasing state and federal funding, stimulated the expansion of the guidance program in the secondary schools, and pushed for the installation of a tuition-free remedial summer program.

I was very pleased when I was given the honor of holding the special chrome-plated symbolic shovel at the groundbreaking for Dedham High's new addition.

When I was re-elected, without opposition, to another three-year term I backed away from consideration as Chairman for the coming year. I felt that I had experienced more than enough of that kind of leadership position.

Actually, I felt exhausted by my own success. The collective bargaining negotiations had drained a lot of my psychic energy because we had done our own negotiating without the help of a professional consultant. That was a mistake that was remedied in succeeding years.

Unfortunately, the Dedham Teachers' Association that had been friendly before our collective bargaining became an adversary with one "demand" after another. I found the process annoying and this was a factor in my decision to consider parting company with the local political process.

At this time, I was being encouraged by some key folks in Dedham to run for office at the state level. But I came to the conclusion that politics was not my choice for a satisfying way of life. So I declined the offers.

As my five-year point with the Chevy Dealers began to

creep closer, I believe I was in the early years of what some people describe as a mid-life crisis. So I was evaluating my life to date, trying to map out where I might be headed.

I concluded that I was not satisfied with my direction, even though our family now had a measure of material success and I was attracting some personal recognition.

Regardless of my material success, I knew I needed to give more energy to my fiction writing. So, in 1968, at age 36, I resigned from the Dedham School Committee after a year into my second term, and concentrated on my writing.

At that time an ambitious *Boston Globe* journalist invited me to lunch in Boston and grilled me about why I had left the Committee. I made the error of assuming that some of our casual conversation over lunch was off the record.

When I told him that several of my remarks were off the record, he said the request to be off the record must come before a statement, not later. I didn't like his attitude but I learned from it. Yes, my candid remarks about leaving the School Committee were published by him in the *Globe*.

At that time in my life the following old saying became a factor: "Life is what happens while you are making other plans." My personal life in the late 1960s became very challenging, to put it mildly.

My marriage had always been important to me, but my

wife and I were now having persistent problems and becoming extremely alienated from each other.

This friction led to an unusual experience one evening after extended arguing. I found myself screaming and crying a torrent of tears uncontrollably. That precipitated an out-of-body experience.

Feeling despair and total exhaustion, I actually let go of life and found myself far above my own body, looking down at my lifeless form on the bed. Functioning as a spirit and separated from my body, I was in a place beyond life.

For a brief time, I believe my body was dead. But I was aware that I still had a choice. I could leave my body in its lifeless state or I could return to it. I decided to return, and that decision was based on curiosity.

I was curious about what was going to happen with my marriage, my children, my work, my friends, and my life. So I returned to my body and continued to function with a much freer feeling because I had made the choice to live.

A Taste of Paradise in Ogunquit, Maine

During this period that included material success, I was motivated to buy a second home a few yards from the ocean on Shore Road next to the Museum of Art in Ogunquit, Maine. The name of the community had come from the

Native Americans and it meant "Beautiful Place by the Sea."

To finance the real estate venture, I proposed to the Chevy Dealers that instead of the usual pay raise I would like to receive the money in the form of a bonus. They agreed and that gave me the funds to make the down payment on the cottage. We bought the cottage for about $16,000. Decades later, a subsequent owner offered it up for sale at a price of more than one million. But that's another story.

The cottage was on the ocean side of Shore Road between the art museum and Juniper Lane. The York/Ogunquit Town Line actually went through our acreage and practically up to the detached garage that I converted into a writing studio.

Just a few weeks in Maine during that summer of '68 proved to be medicine for the ill health I had been experiencing. From the time of my marriage at age 21 until age 34, my health had been in fairly good balance except for some difficult bouts with virus infections. But now I was afflicted by irritable bowel syndrome, borderline diabetes, and hypertension, along with the chronic fatigue that had always haunted me.

The stress of my life in 20th Century America had caught up with my sensitive nervous system. My spirit was out of balance too. As I reflect back on that time, it is apparent that as I had become more successful in the material world, I had also been less spiritually inclined.

In those days I even wondered if God had turned his attention elsewhere in the galaxy instead of our planet. I was thinking more like an agnostic, but additional adversity would soon move me into a closer relationship with God.

Our first summer in the cottage next to artist Henry Strater's Museum of Art of Ogunquit was a turning point for us. This period away from the stress, racial tension, and rioting in Boston in the late 1960s was all we needed to motivate us to move from Dedham to the Maine coast.

We sold our house in Dedham, paid off the mortgage in Maine, and relocated. But I needed to work out a deal with the Chevy Dealers that would enable me to live in Maine and still handle the affairs of the association.

Independent Management Consultant

Approaching the end of my fourth year with the Chevrolet Dealers Association in 1968, I proposed another work arrangement. I would serve them as their independent management consultant at two-thirds of my previous full-time schedule, with an appropriate reduction in pay.

Based on my proposal, I would handle most of the work I had done as Executive Director, and we would move their office from Boston's South Shore in Braintree to the North

Shore of Massachusetts. This would give me an easy commute from my new home base in southern Maine.

The board of directors accepted my plan. Then we worked out a contract for one year at a time which could be terminated on 90 days notice each year by either me or the dealers. In an additional move toward my independence, I bought the company car, a Chevrolet Bel Air wagon, for a very affordable price.

Within a matter of weeks, I relocated the Association office to Danvers, north of Boston. Then I began commuting back and forth from our cottage in Maine to Danvers, using a secretarial bureau there in lieu of office staff. The commute was a little over an hour. And I began to feel very free.

Ironically, without intending to do so, I was moving toward fulfilling the idea of the dealer who had told me he wanted to eliminate my role as Executive Director. I was actually heading in that direction voluntarily.

My actions were linked to my own imperative to be as free as I could be and still survive economically. Individual freedom has always been one of my highest values, in great part due to having spent nine years in Mrs. White's Catholic Charities group home where freedom was severely limited.

Freedom was an issue for the village of Ogunquit too. At the time when we relocated to Ogunquit it was a village within the boundaries of the Town of Wells. Some years later the village, after many years of legal maneuvering, managed to secede from Wells. The celebration, with fireworks on the beach, was exhilarating. The village was setting itself free to make its own decisions.

In Ogunquit, Mary began painting portraits and also gave piano lessons. Our three daughters made a smooth transition to the Wells, Maine school system. I had trimmed down the duties of my job with the Chevy dealers, so I had an abundance of available time for writing novels and essays.

Life in Maine was very special. From our property near Perkins Cove we could see through the glass of the museum to the rocks bordering Narrow Cove and the ocean. This portion of the coastline was awe-inspiring and stimulating.

It seemed at first that I was a modern Great Gatsby and we were moving forward with destiny in our Ogunquit Paradise. But maybe our wishful thinking was more in line with the G.B. Shaw play Too True to Be Good. Yet wasn't it good to have only one debt-free house to care for now?

Very soon it would again be time to consider my five-year plan. Was I losing interest in being the front man for the Chevy Dealers? Sure I was. I had a natural cycle when it came to working for others. At first, there was the burst of enthusiasm for the new enterprise. Then there was the period of building. Inevitably the plateau arrived. Eventually, there would be a downhill decline in my interest.

At that point I would tend to be afflicted by minor irritations. And my resistance to arbitrary authority would stimulate large resentments in my highly imaginative mind. But over the years, time after time, when I gave my notice that I would be leaving a job the irritations would disappear, as if by magic, and I would no longer be concerned with the details or the people that seemed so irksome before.

The year of my Chevy Dealers contract went by fast and soon I had to decide on my connection with the dealers. I chose to stick to my five-year master plan, so in September I gave 90 days notice that I was terminating our arrangement, effective December 31, 1968. It was mutually agreed.

When it came to employment, I had climbed out on a tree limb and then sawed almost all the way through the fiscal branch that supported me and my wife and three daughters. I had very little in the checking account and no savings. Yet I trusted that despite the risks that went with terminating my employment contract, things would turn out well.

Wouldn't the Lord provide? Of course, but I needed to do the footwork to accomplish the employment goal. As Mrs. White had often said, "The Lord helps those that help themselves."

12.
BACK TO CLAIMS REPRESENTATIVE
Seek and ye shall find (God Calling)

Crum & Forster Insurance Company

Because my contract with the Chevy Dealers would expire at the end of December, it was time to look for work in Maine and New Hampshire. And jobs were hard to find.

It is amazing how fast money disappears when you are running out of it. The suspense built and no substantial leads emerged. At that time there seemed to be no opportunities in Maine or nearby New Hampshire for a person with my organizational and communication skills.

I came from a generation in which the man was the breadwinner and the wife was manager of the household. Mary's income from her creative pursuits was minor compared to the amount necessary to keep us afloat. So I was running out of options.

For the first time in my adult life, my latest self-propelled downward mobility was rushing me toward unemployment. Finally, I decided to see if I could revert to claims work and utilize my five years with Amica as a claims investigator.

I began sending my resume to insurance carriers north of

Boston and that decision paid off. I attracted the interest of Crum & Forster Insurance Company which had a Portland, Maine branch. They called me in to be interviewed. The interview went very well. Then, as the end of my contract with the Chevy Dealers loomed closer and closer, I waited…and prayed…for the Crum & Forster decision.

At the eleventh hour, just before Christmas, the phone call came. They had decided to hire me. My position would start effective January 1, 1969, and I would be the Crum & Forster Claims Representative for Maine and New Hampshire, operating out of Portland. This was a big relief.

The job provided a new company car, the freedom of only needing to spend one day a week in Portland at my desk in the office there, and a pace that suited my temperament.

Crum & Forster was a major insurance carrier, including coverage for vehicles, homes, and commercial enterprises such as the produce of Aroostook County potato farmers in Northern Maine.

I personally investigated mostly auto and a few home owners claims in Southern Maine and nearby New Hampshire. When a claim exceeded my own ability to handle it, I would assign it to the General Adjustment Bureau or another private claims adjustment organization.

While on the road I would also visit local insurance

agents. In those days Amica wrote policies directly and did not utilize agents, whereas Crum & Forster relied strongly on its network of local insurance agencies.

I was not directly handling claims resulting from fires in potato barns in Aroostook County. But I heard stories about those "baked potato" cases from the personnel in our Portland office. Arson had to be considered as a matter for thorough investigation before settling potato barn claims.

Handling claims in northern New England was interesting work. And it gave me renewed energy and time for other pursuits. To see if I might enjoy teaching part-time at the college level, I applied locally.

My application was accepted by New Hampshire College in Manchester. Soon I was teaching both Fundamentals of Logic and Introduction to Philosophy as a member of the adjunct faculty at the college's nearby Portsmouth Center.

Each semester was condensed into eight weeks and the classes were four hours long. It was a bit of an endurance test but I appreciated the opportunity to teach at the college level.

While living in Maine I also wrote novels and solicited publishers without success. Eventually, I found a highly respected literary agent in New York. Howard Moorepark appreciated my work and did his best to sell it but was unable to do that for me despite what he called "its merits."

My lack of literary success prodded me to go on writing…and on…and on. But it was depressing to write fiction and not sell it. This surely had its impact on my sensitive frame of mind.

Adding to the negative side of the ledger was the fact that our marriage was still not going well. One reason for moving to Maine had been to improve our marriage. Paradoxically, at our new location in one of the most beautiful settings on the planet, things got worse. Trouble in Paradise.

Therefore, to help myself cope with life, I was using more alcohol plus doses of valium. Alcohol is a depressant drug and even though valium had a calming effect, it had a tendency to depress the psyche. So, as I reflect on life in the late 1960s and early 1970s I can see that I was suffering from ongoing depression but living in denial about it.

Another event complicated the situation. I had a shocking setback in my health. One morning I woke up feeling very strange and when I looked in the bathroom mirror prior to shaving I saw that my left eye was frozen in a wide open position and my mouth was greatly distorted.

The left side of my face felt the way it feels after having Novocain at the dentist. And I was drooling. It looked to me as if I had experienced a stroke. I could neither close my left eye nor use the left side of my mouth, and the frightening symptoms lingered for weeks.

Finally, a visit to the Lahey Clinic in Boston brought a verdict of "Bell's Palsy," a condition affecting a cranial nerve. Very slowly, my face returned to normal. I was fortunate. I have known others with the same condition who had to wear eye patches for the rest of their lives.

Although I had been terrified by the situation, it prompted me to write myself an inspirational essay that reflected on the difficulties of life. I expressed my deep belief in God, and accepted everything that had ever happened to me. Adversity was bringing me closer to God again

As for our family, a shining ray of light came to us on June 20, 1970, when our son Sean Thomas O'Connell was born at nearby Portsmouth Hospital in New Hampshire. He was greeted with joy by his three sisters, his mother and me.

However, even with Sean's joyful presence, our marriage was in dire straits. From my perspective our Maine winters resembled some scenes in Tolstoy's novel *Anna Karenina*.

For Mary and I to spend large amounts of time with each other seemed to be toxic to us. Or perhaps I should say we became allergic to each other. Asking God's help in prayer, we decided that it was time to move back to Massachusetts.

Then what? What kind of work would I do in the Boston area? Claims? Public relations? Association management?

13.
CEO: TENANTS POLICY COUNCIL
Life is a training school (God Calling)

Boston Public Housing Tenants Policy Council

The answer to my employment questions came when I saw an ad in the Boston papers. An Executive Director was needed for Boston's public housing tenants organization.

I believed that my years as a staff executive with the Massachusetts Safety Council followed by five years of association management with the Chevrolet Dealers Association would be assets.

So I entered into competition with about 100 other applicants. As the years passed, based on newspaper ads, the competition for various jobs I was seeking or positions I wanted to fill always seemed to average 100 applicants.

After a battery of interviews with committees and the Board of Directors itself, I was selected to be leader and spokesperson for the privately funded nonprofit organization called Boston Public Housing Tenants Policy Council (TPC).

The Council represented Boston's 55,000 public housing tenants in its basic mission to improve living conditions for the tenants. Most of them lived in the housing projects throughout the city. Others lived in various neighborhoods.

The TPC maintained offices at 99 Bedford Street in the central city near South Station and China Town. In my role as Executive Director, I reported to a large and unwieldy board of forty-two directors of varying ethnicity who represented the many public housing projects sprinkled throughout the city. There were so many minority folks on my board, I recall feeling embarrassed that I was so white.

Funding for the organization came primarily from charitable foundations, especially Boston's Permanent Charity Fund. An important part of my job was to maintain the flow of financial support and attempt to expand it.

As I have said before, life is what happens while you are making other plans. My TPC role was a hectic job involving Boston politics and I had only a very small office staff. You might say I had a three-ring circus on my hands and I was the ringmaster of all three rings.

I soon learned about the flaws in public housing as I visited the projects, met with members of my Board of Directors, and actually sat at the long table as ad hoc tenant representative (without a vote) in meetings of the Commissioners of the Boston Housing Authority (BHA).

Also, I represented the tenants in battles with City Hall where Mayor Kevin White presided, and I did liaison work with state and federal officials.

On one occasion, my Board of Directors asked me to represent the TPC at a meeting of the Boston City Council where they would be discussing nominations to a high position in public housing.

When I got on the stand under oath, Councilman Dapper O'Neil, a legendary character in Boston politics, took his turn at questioning me. I was not ready for the kind of third degree he arranged for me.

Obviously, his tactic was to degrade me to a point where I would have no credibility. Relentlessly, he proceeded to remove my right to any kind of privacy about my job.

"Where do you live, Mr. O'Connell?"

"Dedham."

"And you are the Executive Director of the Boston Public Housing Tenants Policy Council? How can that be?"

"I was chosen for the job by the TPC Board of Directors who represent the tenants in Boston's housing projects."

"What do you know about public housing?"

"I lived in a veterans' housing project in Dedham for years. In my current job I meet with tenants in the various projects and participate in meetings of the Commissioners of the Boston Housing Authority."

"By what authority do you appear before the Boston City

Council?"

This was the way it went. It felt like I was being publicly undressed for the sole purpose of humiliating me. This was not paranoia; this was city politics. His questions about my salary touched on areas of my personal life that I considered totally private, but I was under oath and there seemed to be no way to escape. This was Boston politics at its worst, as far as I was concerned. But it went with the territory.

Despite similar challenges while serving as the leader of the TPC I was able to help the organization resolve one of their key issues. I coordinated a unified campaign to enact a precedent-setting lease and grievance procedure spelling out tenants' rights and the Housing Authority's obligations.

To accomplish this goal, I led delegations of tenants and their politically active leaders to BHA meetings. With this persistence, the Boston Housing Authority finally passed a landmark lease which spelled out tenants' rights for the first time and also provided a grievance mechanism.

To further the organizational goal of improving living conditions in Boston's public housing, I also waged mass media campaigns to enhance public awareness of life in the city's housing projects.

Obviously, my basic love of mass media communication moved with me from job to job and was a vital part of my organizational focus. I also worked consistently on internal communications with the housing projects, attending their meetings throughout the city.

My tenure with the Council was brief, less than a year, because shortly after I began working at TPC the main source of funding dried up. During the interview process, I had been led to believe that the Permanent Charity Fund would continue to provide most of the funding. But when I visited the prestigious foundation I learned otherwise. I was told that their commitment had been just for start-up funding and that period would soon end.

Although I only served briefly with the Boston Public Housing Tenants Policy Council, it was an action-packed time resembling in intensity the months politicians have to spend as they lead up to a major election. To say that the job was exhausting would be a major understatement.

When I met with Mayor White privately to sound him out on key issues, he made it very clear that he had minimal interest in Boston's 55,000 public housing tenants. Why? He simply told me that it was because he didn't have a majority of the votes of the BHA Commissioners in his pocket.

Without using the expletives he utilized to spice up his private comments, I have to say that Kevin White gave me very candid responses to my questions. He certainly did not pretend to be a great humanitarian. Clearly, he was a politician at his core, thought like one, and operated like one.

Nevertheless, despite the Mayor's uncooperative positions on various issues related to public housing, I was able to arrange forums at City Hall for the tenants to express themselves. Also, I worked to expand communication with government, the public, and the members of the tenant organization.

As my last official act, I organized a highly publicized fact finding tour of Boston's housing projects by U.S. Senator Edward Brooke. At some of the projects included in his tour, their streets with broken glass looked like the photos of heavily bombed German cities following World War II. It was useful to expose this reality for public awareness.

At this juncture, with the impending loss of funding from the Boston Public Housing Tenants Policy Council's major means of support, there was no other possibility except for me to bail out at a short distance from the ground, pray for a favorable outcome, and trust that my employment parachute would open before I hit solid earth.

Once again, prayer helped me to maintain my sense of spiritual security as any semblance of material security was rapidly disappearing.

14.
CEO: MASS. FEDERATION OF NURSING HOMES
Never count success by money gained (God Calling)

Massachusetts Federation of Nursing Homes

My next job search took me into competition with about 100 other applicants for the role of Executive Director of the Massachusetts Federation of Nursing Homes. It happened to be headquartered in my hometown of Dedham.

I won the contest, but three months later when the search committee's second choice visited me, I told him, "Jim, when you didn't get this job, you were very lucky. The intensity is beyond belief." That job gave me some of the most stressful and fatiguing years of my adult life, ranking along with my two years in the Army.

From 1972 to 1975, as Executive Director of the trade association representing more than 300 nursing homes and other healthcare facilities in Massachusetts, one of my most important functions was to expand government relations and organize legislative activity leading to governmental agency reorganization at the state level.

I became a registered lobbyist at the State House and took guidance from highly skilled professional lobbyists hired by the Federation. Among other things, I coordinated a dynamic campaign to persuade Governor Frank Sargent to enact a deficiency budget to pay some 70 million dollars in overdue obligations to health care providers in the Bay State. This was easier said than done because the Governor had made a pledge to file no deficiency budgets that year.

With valuable assistance from President Charles Kelley and other leaders of the Federation, I organized a coalition of key people in the health care field to pursue this goal. The strategy using considerable mass media and lobbying was successful, but I was exhausted beyond description.

Maybe the Governor was exhausted too as he signed the legislation enacting the deficiency budget. I recall posing for the photographer at the signing ceremony in his office with other health care leaders.

As we lined up behind Governor Sargent who was at his desk I decided impulsively to lean over and whisper in his ear. I boldly asked him about how much progress he was making on another piece of legislation important to the health care sector.

I will always remember how his face reddened angrily as he looked up at me and muttered a noncommittal response. I had stepped over a boundary. The man who presented a good natured personality to the public had a formidable side. The unwritten message on his face as he gazed at me was, "Don't mess with Governor Frank Sargent."

In the lobby outside the Governor's office at another time I was involved in a TV interview I have never forgotten. This took place after I had put together a small crowd to apply pressure to "the man in the corner office," which is how the Governor is described at the State House.

Dick Flavin, a veteran TV newscaster in Boston, was interviewing me and asked a very long question. I was tempted to give a witty answer because while he was dominating the interview my mind was elsewhere.

I kept thinking of the Bob and Ray comedy team and their funny radio skits in which they would ask an athlete a long question and have him give a one-word response. To avoid that outcome I decided to paraphrase Flavin's question by repeating words he had just used. That solved my problem.

Beyond my work in the legislative process, I stimulated more educational programs for nursing home personnel, promoted higher ethical standards, developed visibility for the industry in the broadcast media, and created newsletters and Sunday supplements in the Boston newspapers to enhance the image of long-term health care facilities.

I did not love politics and had thought I was done with it after serving on the Dedham School Committee, and being immersed in Boston politics with the public housing tenants. But the demands of my new post as Executive Director transformed me into a political coalition organizer, media campaign tactician, and health care leader at the State level.

Also, due to my new status as a registered lobbyist at the State House, I was working with some of the most experienced professional lobbyists on "the Hill" who counseled me on strategy.

However, I was once again pressing my luck with my health, and I began to feel deeply "burned out" physically and emotionally. Along with the intensity of the job, my marital life was steadily deteriorating.

Although I kept working on my novels and had outstanding literary agents from New York City and Beverly Hills representing me, my books were still unpublished.

Florence Feiler on the west coast was agent for the Isak Dinesen estate and the rights to the book and film *Out of Africa*. But as much as she said she admired my fiction she was unable to find a publisher for it.

Another problem during this time was my work in the political arena, based on the art of compromise. I began to feel like a man walking a tightrope between two high buildings, one with the sign "Survival and Success" and the other with the sign "Pitfalls of Ambition." I did not appreciate that feeling.

One major challenge was a nursing home owner who had been trained in the tactics of the political agitator Saul Alinsky in Chicago. This Alinsky disciple was attempting to apply Chicago style to our Massachusetts strategy. His approach was not illegal, so this put me somewhere between a rock and a hard place, as they say.

I recall having some high noon "shoot-outs" with this gentleman before large meetings of our membership. In some respects I was setting myself up for his challenges. But I felt I had to have the courage to face up to my adversary.

After I had a public duel with this guy, a member of our Board of Directors said to me, "You've got a lot of balls, Tom. You really let him have it." I was not proud of my extremely aggressive acting performance, but I felt I had no choice. As for my adversary, he simply kept escalating his challenges aimed at me and my staff.

Furthering my political education, the Alinsky disciple won approval to bring in some additional political "experts" to guide our association into successful activity. These were folks who had served as "political operatives" in national Democratic campaigns.

They were hardcore operatives, and to know them was to lose respect for them. One of their favorite words was "neutralize." This meant that if anyone got in their way and messed with their objectives they would try tactics designed to reduce the person to political impotence.

Even with arms length contact, I found these people hazardous to my emotional health. However, a business recession was in process, jobs were scarce at the level I had achieved, and I saw no way out of the situation.

On the plus side, I was paid well enough to push me into higher levels of the middle class, and I was able to take business-related all-expense paid trips with Mary to beautiful spots such as Hawaii and England. I enjoyed the trips.

The two trips to Hawaii were to attend annual conferences of the national organization representing the nursing homes of the United States. Similar meetings also exposed me to San Francisco, New Orleans, Dallas, Atlanta, Chicago, and other U. S. cities. I found this travel very educational.

The trip to England came my way because I was on the Board of Directors of New England Society of Association Executives. As leaders who were likely to need conference facilities, we were invited to take an all-expense paid tour of the best hotel and conference facilities in England.

It was the ultimate junket. We were wined and dined in very upscale hotels such as the internationally known Grosvenor House in London and other fine facilities. One exceptional facility was a former castle out in the countryside that had been converted into a luxurious conference center for corporate executives and others.

We were told that the original lady of the manor had looked out a window in her castle one day, didn't like the appearance of the village nearby, and ordered the village moved so she would have an uninterrupted view.

In spite of the lavish nature of the junket to England, as I have noted before, the years have taught me that various pleasures and successes in my life have always carried a price. My body and psyche have been relatively unconcerned with success and instead have preferred a moderate pace, creative satisfaction, and balance.

Eventually, I visited my family physician, a brilliant M.D. and Osteopath. Dr. Blanke was superb at diagnoses. His verdict was summed up in two words: "Nervous exhaustion." My aorta was giving off loud sounds. My ears felt flushed and ultra-sensitive. Adding to my anxieties, a skin cancer developed behind my right ear. I was terrified.

One stress after another built at this time and I was beginning to feel like the living embodiment of the mythological Sisyphus who was doomed to keep rolling a huge rock up a hill, only to have it roll back down, forcing him to keep pushing it back up again...without end.

A beloved uncle was dying of cancer. My wife was getting involved in auto accidents and threatening to separate from me. And I was stricken by a viral infection that left me feeling dangerously weak from the waist down.

It was as if an electrical switch had been thrown, cutting off a vital supply of my limited energy. I have observed over the years that when it comes to physical energy, people's limits vary considerably. The limits range all the way from very low energy to very high. As I have noted before, I have never had a high level of physical energy and instead I have had a vast reservoir of brain energy.

At this juncture, in my work with the long term health care facilities and their government relations, my brain and central nervous system energy were being challenged. So I had a ponderously heavy burden of holistic exhaustion haunting me. This burden, when added to the chronic physical fatigue I had carried with me through much of my life, was now oppressive at almost unbearable levels.

Suffering from chronic fatigue and sadness, I nevertheless organized great legislative victories and was a mass media personality. Also, I attracted the recognition of my peers, and served on boards of directors of professional societies.

However, there was something fundamentally wrong. I was successful yet I felt trapped by my own life. My marriage was becoming much less of a marriage. My creative writing goals had not paid off except in some very minor ways. So I felt I was not measuring up to my own hopes and dreams when it came to family happiness and personal creativity.

Adversity again proved helpful to me, because in the midst of my suffering I discovered the work of psychologist Carl Jung. I found explanations in his writings that helped me in my own search for meaning in my life. I could relate to Jung's thinking, and I credit his work with getting me to see life from a more healthy perspective.

I especially appreciated his 1955 book *Modern Man in Search of a Soul* and his 1957 book *The Undiscovered Self.* Also, to improve my understanding of Jung's work I took a course in Jungian Psychology at Curry College in Milton where Professor Fran MacPherson inspired me.

With the help of my Jungian studies, I began to look deeply into my own soul. Then it became obvious that I had to part company with the nursing home association and change the direction I was following.

I started looking for a college teaching job as a way to bail out after three years of exhausting intensity in the field of long term health care. I thought I might find a workplace "home" in the field of higher education, having experienced some of that more satisfying way of life while in Maine, teaching Logic and Philosophy at New Hampshire College.

With high level contacts at the State House, I was able to meet very influential people in higher education. While I explored the possibility of shifting to an academic career, one high ranking educator said to me, "With your vast experience, you are either a candidate for a special award or a heart attack!" It was not my destiny to receive either one.

Soon it became obvious to me that full-time faculty openings at the college level were few and far between. Also, the entry pay level was nowhere near what I needed to meet obligations. How did I feel at this time? Like a man on a dead end street with no visible exit.

Right at that time, however, a friend told me he had heard about the coming retirement of the current Chief Executive Officer of the Massachusetts Safety Council, where I had served as Public Information Director ten years earlier.

It sounded like a perfect opportunity for me to pursue... with whatever guidance the Lord might provide. So I intensified my prayer life.

15.
CEO: MASSACHUSETTS SAFETY COUNCIL
Be filled with sublime audacity (God Calling)

Massachusetts Safety Council Leader

The screening process for the Safety Council job was almost over when I entered the competition. But there I was, once again competing for another Chief Executive position.

This time I was familiar with the organization, and I was optimistic about returning to accident prevention. The Council had moved its offices from Devonshire Street to an ideal location on Beacon Street at the top of Beacon Hill. It was up above Goodspeed's Book Shop and across from the long wide steps of the front entrance to the State House.

However, as I was about to take the elevator up to the higher level where the Mass. Safety Council's Executive Committee was going to interview me, an ominous event took place. I began to feel amazingly weak, with symptoms similar to the flu. It was the feeling of having "a pit in my stomach" and weak legs. But I decided to ignore the feeling.

As my future unfolded at the Safety Council I often recalled that feeling and thought of it as an ignored omen. When the screening was finished a few weeks later I had the job, and feeling a bit like Rip Van Winkle, I went back to head up the organization I had left a decade before.

In 1975 at age 43 I was appointed CEO of the Massachusetts Safety Council, Inc., and once again had the mission of preventing accidents on the highways, in the home, and in the workplace. In a short time, I felt recharged with energy and set ambitious goals for the organization.

I also inherited a staff of executives and a crew of secretarial/clerical personnel to nurture. This was a challenge for me. I had learned in other leadership positions that the folks I inherited often thought of me as a new stepfather. Their loyalty was with the guy I had replaced. Staff who showed the most loyalty were those I hired myself.

I had learned that my self-taught management-by-exception style suited people who liked to work independently. But those who enjoyed having their superiors closely supervise them had difficulty adjusting to a freedom loving independent character such as myself.

Management-by-exception simply means that as a boss I tried to avoid sticking my nose into the business of those who worked under my authority. But on the other hand, I promised that if something was proving hard to handle all staff were encouraged to come to me for help.

Most of the time, I left my office door open. Therefore,

when it was closed my colleagues knew it was not a good time to interrupt the boss. Yes, again I was a boss. And this time I was leading a very prestigious organization.

My private office was very large and through a huge bay window I had a spectacular view of the glistening golden dome of the State House. As I sat there in a swivel chair I could spin between two desks.

One desk faced the bay window and the golden view. The other desk had a massive conference table extending out from it so that we could hold small meetings there. And the table gave me plenty of space to spread out paper work.

To achieve the Council's goals, I attracted new funding from the auto insurance industry for media campaigns on the need to support the 55 mph speed limit. We started with the slogan "55 Will Get You There…Safer, Cheaper, Calmer." After a while we just said, "55 Will Get You There." My campaign attracted attention both regionally and nationally.

Much later, I launched a dynamic highway courtesy campaign that carried the slogan, "A Little Courtesy Won't Kill You." Due to the nature of my work, I became a highly visible spokesperson in the news and information media.

I was a regular guest on major Boston area TV and radio talk shows and news features. Also, I was featured in many public service commercials funded by proposals I devised and successfully presented to the auto insurance industry.

There was much satisfaction in the position I held. It seemed for a while to be the kind of place where I might stay for a long time, right into retirement. I might even be tempted to abandon my concept of five-year plans.

Around this time I was appointed to the Governor's Highway Safety Committee under Governor Mike Dukakis. Also, I served on the Executive Committee of National Safety Council's Conference of State and Local Safety Organizations in Chicago. And I enjoyed presenting awards to outstanding Massachusetts citizens for supporting vital life-saving accident prevention activities.

An objective observer might have said that I had a lot going for me at the time. I had earned a widespread reputation as a crusader in the public interest, received constant recognition locally, and even gained attention at the national level for the kinds of campaigns I was waging in Massachusetts.

The boy from the other side of the tracks, in the shadow of the East Dedham railroad station, had risen to great heights. We had our family home in Dedham in the middle class Oakdale section of town. Also, we had our place on the Maine coast in Ogunquit next to the Ogunquit Museum of Art, one of the most beautiful locations on the planet.

I was a highly visible figure in one of the nation's major metropolitan areas. And I was able to use my intelligence and creativity in useful ways to benefit the human race. So the world seemed to be my oyster.

I wonder if it seems to readers that I am boasting about my past as I write this memoir. Actually, I am sticking to the facts along with some of my feelings. It's my true story and I have lived it in my own way.

At any rate, when I was at the height of my mass media visibility, the President of the *Boston Globe* Newspaper Company, John Giuggio, approached me at a meeting we were attending in the *Globe's* executive dining room. He noted the extent to which I had become a public figure. Then this fine gentleman commented on the widespread exposure I was receiving throughout the mass media.

He asked seriously, "Would you be interested in running for Governor?"

My quick response required no deliberation. "No, John. Thanks for asking, but I've been over-exposed to politics. That way of life doesn't interest me." The even more candid truth was that the political way of life nauseated me.

My comment to John was sincere. Also, it was brief because he was on my Board of Directors. Discretion was needed. I was not about to tell him at that time that there was something deep inside me that remained uncomfortable with the direction my life was taking, including my leadership of the Massachusetts Safety Council.

My exhausted feeling was constant. Intestinal problems arose. High blood pressure continued. And tears would come into my eyes for no apparent reason. Tranquilizers did not help. Alcohol was no solution because a depressant drug is not an antidote for exhaustion.

Much of the pressure in my life, I am sure, came from within me, based on my inherent existential restlessness. But the marital difficulties intensified. And I was feeling deep animosity from a minority faction on my board of directors.

I had learned in organizational work that no matter how well conceived one's efforts as a leader might be, and no matter how effective one was while moving the organization toward its goals, there would always be people in power on the Board or Executive Committee who felt determined to oppose the leader they had hired. The reasons for their negativity were seldom rational, and could be very annoying.

In those days, while some folks on my Board of Directors good naturedly called me Mr. Safety Council, behind the scenes I had some militant opposition to contend with, and it wore at my patience. I would win battle after battle but I got very tired of fighting the battles.

One illustrious gentleman who was a high level volunteer at the Council adopted the role of "devil's advocate" when it came to any recommendation I would make at an Executive Committee meeting. He was not just an ant at my picnic; he was an irritating mosquito.

He had been away on an extended vacation when I had won the job and by the time he returned I had developed a plan of action for the Safety Council that had been approved by the Executive Committee. The plan placed a high priority on highway safety public information activities.

After getting back from his trip, my new adversary confronted me and told me he was opposed to my plan of action. He arrogantly demanded that I retract it. Also, he indicated that he was more interested in occupational safety and thought that would be a better focus for the Council.

However, I refused to back down. Then he threatened me with a statement indicating that I would live to regret my decision not to go along with him.

For the rest of my time at the Safety Council he held on to his negativity toward me. I tried to respond with detachment but often he managed "to get my Irish up." We Irish are known for not walking away from a fight. And the two of us had Irish backgrounds.

Another interesting part of our mutual antagonism was the

fact that we were both Catholics. We each made visits to the same little chapel on the street leading to the State House which was a short walk from our offices on Beacon Street. To this day, I believe we were both praying for the Lord to vanquish the opposition we were receiving from each other.

I learned much later about the extent of his vindictiveness. Apparently, he was driven to distraction by my successful highway safety public information campaigns. I was told by a reliable source that he had tried to get the head of a leading Boston corporation to hire the man I had recruited to work with me on public information.

That man and I were a terrific team and my adversary did his best to wreck that team but failed. However, he was not a good loser. Instead, he became a permanent thorn in my side throughout my tenure at the Safety Council. This became an ongoing challenge for my status as a practicing Christian. I had to pray constantly for the grace to forgive him.

One day many years after I had left the Council I was in Boston on foot, crossing an intersection near Beacon Street. I saw an old blind man with a white cane waiting to cross. Then I realized it was my former adversary.

I recalled Jesus' counsel that we should love our enemies, so I decided to introduce myself. After having a brief chat I helped him get safely across the street and he thanked me.

As we parted, we shook hands. And that chance meeting seemed to bring a kind of spiritual closure to a very uncomfortable episode in my life.

Although there was much satisfaction to be gained at the Safety Council, administration of any kind had always gone against my grain. Hiring and firing personnel, and needing to supervise them, was definitely not my cup of tea.

I admit that I was more of a creative campaigner than an administrator. I thrived on action that brought results. So it was a debilitating energy drain to deal with adversaries who had nothing better to think about than undermining my efforts on behalf of the Council.

Actually, after my years of serving as CEO of four nonprofit organizations, I believe I was in the advanced stages of career burnout. Also, I had refined the thinking that led to my Target Theory of Leadership.

Four leadership positions had taught me that the person at the top is not only a target, but actually a bull's-eye at the heart of the target. Ouch!

The bull's-eye attracts praise here and there, and money, and often an abundance of prestige. But if the leader is innovative and imaginative he also attracts an ongoing barrage of critical darts from disgruntled Board and committee members, staff executives, secretarial and clerical personnel, and sometimes from sources outside one's organization. I was just plain tired of being a target.

Therefore, in 1978 after much reflection and having had a spiritual awakening, I decided to leave the Massachusetts Safety Council. My key volunteer, President Peter Quinn, and others at the Council tried to talk me into staying but I felt I had to set myself free to move on with my life.

A note here about Peter Quinn, who had led a very successful career in retailing. He was one of the finest gentlemen I have ever known and a source of strength for me in my role as CEO of the Massachusetts Safety Council.

Peter had a combination of intellectual brilliance and inner calmness that was a very steadying influence for me and all those whose lives he touched. He was more than Council President; he was my dependable friend.

However, I knew what I had to do at this stage of my life. At age 46 I needed to move toward heightened individual freedom. It was imperative for me to stop managing other people's organizations as a hired leader.

I had an inner mandate that had to be obeyed. This was expressed so well by William Shakespeare: "To thine own self be true, And it must follow, as the night the day, Thou canst not be false to any man."

At that time my goal was to refine my approach to my

creative writing and also build a new nonprofit organization that I called the Health Information Institute, Inc. The new entity would have a small board of directors that would not be divided by factions. And we would be working on critical health issues not being addressed by others.

I gave the Council six months notice of my departure so there would be time to complete the public information projects I had been working on. This seemed to make sense to me at the time, but such a long goodbye had a downside.

"You're still here? I thought you had resigned." "You haven't gone yet?" "When are you actually leaving?" Some of the questions came under the heading of good natured ribbing. Other people were probably wondering about choosing a successor. But a deal was a deal. So I stuck to it.

The major reason I had given the Council six months notice of my departure was to provide ample time for me to initiate the "A Little Courtesy Won't Kill You" campaign. It was my brainchild and I wanted to get it off to a good start.

I had kicked around the idea of a highway courtesy campaign with my advertising consultant John Dowd who had applied his genius to my campaigns at the Council. And he agreed that it had great merit. John worked with me on funding proposals to the auto insurance carriers of the Bay State and the two of us made a successful creative team.

I conceived the need for a statewide courtesy campaign, but John's creativity was critical in its planning, especially when he helped me hammer out a memorable slogan.

I still have one of the bumper stickers on my car that says, "A Little Courtesy Won't Kill You." It helps me to practice what I preach by being more courteous on the roads myself.

The campaign was very well funded and turned out to be a winner with high impact TV and Radio coverage as well as exposure in the print media. Also, we had our slogan on every Massachusetts auto inspection sticker.

In addition, we distributed thousands of bumper stickers. We even had utility company vehicles throughout the Commonwealth carrying our slogan. And we had bold posters that were distributed widely throughout the State.

With a lot of help from others, I gave that campaign my best shot and still look back on it as one of the highlights of my career in mass media public information.

Obviously, we could still use more highway safety accident prevention campaigns today based on personal courtesy. After all, a courteous attitude makes all the difference in every aspect of life.

I thought it would also be a factor in the new Health Information Institute's birth and future growth. But there were legal technicalities about starting up my new Health

Information Institute. I needed charitable organization status from the IRS which was more complicated than anticipated.

Also, my dear Uncle Joe who was suffering from cancer took a turn for the worse that spring and I was his caretaker. We had to move him from one hospital to another and then I needed to honor his request to relocate him to his cottage in Wells, Maine so that he could die in that beautiful setting on Drakes Island Road. Then we had to arrange for his body to return to Dedham for burial in Brookdale Cemetery.

It was an emotionally grueling experience to deal with all the details of his nursing care and funeral preparations at the very same time that I was leaving the Safety Council and intending to start my new nonprofit organization. Joe died on June 4, 1978 and my departure date from Mass. Safety Council was June 14, Flag Day.

Each year the arrival of Flag Day always reminds me of Joe's death and the day I was given a goodbye celebration by President Peter Quinn and the Board of Directors at the Council's Annual Meeting. An appreciation certificate was given to me at Pier Four restaurant on the Boston waterfront.

That day in 1978 turned out to be my last day of full-time employment. Also, it was the beginning of a new stage in my life. The next stage would be very productive and would expand my personal freedom and creativity.

16
FREELANCE WRITER, LECTURER, EDUCATOR
Be full of gratitude (God Calling)

Freelance Communications Consultant

I put considerable energy into the highway courtesy campaign while at the same time launching the Health Information Institute. However, despite my good intentions I was unable to attract the necessary funding for the new organization and my own financial reserve soon hit bottom.

In good faith, I produced some radio public service announcements and made appearances on radio and TV. During a guest appearance on Channel 5 in Boston for the Institute, my daughter Amy helped me to demonstrate a technique for reducing the severity of elder citizens' falls. But the funding for ongoing activity just didn't materialize.

It is amazing how fast one can plunge from the heights of success and slide into a valley of financial desperation. And that is why I gave this book its title. When a person gets on the upward mobility track it's wise to prepare one's thinking for times of downward mobility too.

Soon after leaving the Council when I had been at the height of success in accident prevention and Boston area fame, I rapidly plummeted into a deep valley of financial distress. Also, I found myself rapidly retreating from my status as a constantly visible media personality.

As I look back at my behavior, it is obvious that God had other plans than the ones I had devised for myself. But I doggedly persisted with the Institute into late 1978, until all of my financial resources had dried up and my mortgage on the house in Dedham was in serious jeopardy.

I was not interested in experiencing another dose of downward mobility, but that is what happened. To get from week to week, I signed on with a temp agency that handled organizations in the Route 128 industrial area near Boston and soon I was earning what I describe as survival pay at rates near the bottom of the income ladder.

One position was with Omni Spectra, an electronics manufacturing organization near Waltham. I was on the night shift and I have vivid memories of how they herded all the temps into a large hall. "You, you and you come with me." This reminded me too much of my years in the U.S. Army, one of the most challenging times of my life.

I didn't appreciate the method used as we were marched along a corridor to a very long room with a set of benches. Then, after a one-minute training program I found myself sitting in front of three small boxes about six inches square.

One box was the incoming box of small metal parts. Another box was marked "minus." The third box was marked "plus."

I was supposed to check each part in a measuring device and based on the result I needed to drop the part into the appropriate box. After doing this for a couple of hours I was bleary eyed, my brain was scrambling, and I found myself dropping the parts into the wrong boxes and realizing that a trained monkey could be more suited for the job than I was.

When it came time for the "lunch" break I just took my lunch bag and kept on walking until I left the building and wished Omni Spectra goodbye with a wave of my hand as I made my exit. I didn't ask for my pay. I simply bugged out.

Also, I decided that I should apply for unemployment benefits even though this did not fit in with my independent way of thinking and functioning. Soon I went to the Norwood office of the State employment security agency and stood in a long line waiting to be processed.

This procedure also reminded me of my "processing" as a private in the U. S. Army. But what else was I to do at this juncture with no savings and no income? Yet the idea was so repugnant to me that before the line reached the main counter I faded away from the line and returned to the great outdoors on the sidewalk. I had opted out.

Instead, I fixed my mind on pursuing individual freedom

and trusted that sufficient income would be provided by guidance from the Lord who was ever present in my heart. I chose to stay with temporary employment for the time being and told myself to avoid feeling panic about the future.

The next temp assignment was with a Polaroid plant near the Norwood/Westwood town line, in the quality control department. The plant was located near the site of the Forbes Estate where Cameron Forbes, the former Governor General of the Philippines, once lived. This was where we used to "borrow" apples from the wonderful orchard there when I was a boy at Mrs. White's Catholic Charities home.

Unlike Omni Spectra, I did a better job of adapting to the lifestyle in that Polaroid factory. There was a relaxed atmosphere, a regular pattern of hours, and predictability about the job. I could see why others could remain in such a work setting for many years. Polaroid was worker friendly.

I recall the skepticism I received when I told some of my fellow workers that I had left a job as CEO of the Safety Council to launch my own enterprise. They thought I was fabricating the whole story. "Right, Tom. Yeah, sure."

A few months later, however, when I gave my notice that I would soon take on my first freelance communications client, Tufts/New England Medical Center in Boston, I think they were more ready to believe me.

This period in my work life was additional confirmation of the tea bag label that had informed me, "Life is what happens while you are making other plans."

It was also a time when I deepened my walk with God. During 1979 I entered a time of preparation at the Arch Street Shrine in Boston operated by the Franciscans. My year of study about the life of Saint Francis of Assisi was the prelude to becoming a Secular Franciscan in 1980, one who is "in the world but not of the world." I have been a Catholic Christian Franciscan ever since. And it has certainly helped me to adjust to God's life-changing plans for my existence.

Back to my tale about work. Having become allergic to working with committees of all kinds, I was determined not to return to Chief Executive work in voluntary associations. Then a twist of fate led me into a reluctant decision to become a communications consultant to nonprofit health and human service organizations.

A grant I had sought from the Massachusetts Commission for the Blind had come very close to being approved. My new organization, the Health Information Institute, was designated as the runner-up.

On the strength of that, a key person at that agency recommended to Tufts/New England Medical Center that they hire me as a consultant to handle a media project for a division working with paraplegics.

With Tufts as my first freelance client, I began soliciting new work with health and human service organizations. Within six months I had as many clients as I could handle, was earning as much money as I had received at the Safety Council, and I had the freedom of managing my own affairs.

Around the same time, the Commission for the Blind used me as a freelance to assist with creation of various brochures and public service messages for radio and TV.

Since parting company with the Mass. Safety Council, I have never worked a full-time schedule with any business. In other words, as Clark Gable commented on "working for wages" in his last film "The Misfits" (1961), I have not worked for full-time "wages" since Flag Day, June 14, 1978. Instead, as the character in Gable's film had chosen to do, I became a confirmed freelance misfit.

Freedom has always been more important to me than financial security and workplace conformity. But it's hard to achieve personal freedom without sacrifices. Some people live in makeshift tents in the woods because they are determined to avoid work slavery. They see a steady salary as a hindrance, not a benefit. I am a lot like those people.

Now, as a freelance, I was embarked on a journey based on my own skill and talents. My expertise as a mass media campaigner, freelance writer, and editorial consultant led me to assignments with many United Way organizations, and I was able to learn much about the inner workings of a wide range of health and human service enterprises.

During the late 1970s and up to the 1990s I worked with clients such as hospitals, visiting nurse associations, addiction treatment centers, educational entities, lung associations, and family service agencies.

One of my interesting clients was the Albert Einstein Library in Boston, a small nonprofit founded by Sol Quasha who had a lifelong interest in Einstein. We launched a major fund raising initiative that centered on two days of entertainment at Symphony Hall in Boston by Victor Borge, the celebrated pianist and humorist.

The Honorary Chairpersons were Kitty Dukakis; Nobel Prize Winner Sheldon Glashow; Tufts University President Dr. Jean Mayer; and Astronomer Carl Sagan.

I was responsible for mass media relations. When the planning committee including renowned scientists was choosing a date for the event, I counseled against the month of March because of possible snowstorms.

They confidently ignored my advice and just as the event opened we had a major blizzard. Also, Pavarotti was in town at the same time. So we had many empty seats at Symphony

Hall. The event didn't even break even and barely avoided pushing the small organization into total oblivion.

However, it was very interesting to work with Victor Borge. He was a funny man onstage and off. We got President Saunders of the Park Plaza Hotel to donate his own suite to Victor who sauntered into the suite, flipped open a closet door, saw the owner's clothing, and said as if offended, "What's this? Somebody's been living here."

Then, at dinner when the Hotel's key man wined and dined us in the newly decorated dining area, he asked Victor how he liked the refurbished facilities. Victor said, "It's fine, but the problem is that your hotel is in the wrong place. It should be across the street from the Public Garden." That was where the Ritz Carlton was located.

Victor helped me to attract major publicity for the event. His fame and his availability made my job easy. And his sense of outrageous fun didn't even stop while he was being interviewed by TV news and Radio teams from the major media outlets.

At Symphony Hall there are little alcoves built into some of the walls. It's where they place statues. While the media people were trying to get his attention, Victor found an empty spot and decided to leap up and fill it with his own body. He could not overlook any humorous possibility.

Despite our blizzard of publicity, the real blizzard won out over the media coverage. It was a terrible storm perfectly timed to provide a box office disaster.

Later on, I had better luck with a similar event in warm weather at Symphony Hall featuring blind jazz legend George Shearing. That event was sponsored by a national organization representing the interests of the blind. I was selected as their Boston area public information practitioner.

For several years I served as communications consultant for the American Lung Association of Massachusetts and other local lung associations of the Greater Boston area, including the Boston group.

Among a host of other public communication activities, I had the responsibility for organizing the annual Christmas Seal Campaign kickoff at the Sheraton Boston Hotel. This included attracting honorary chairperson celebrities such as Miss Teenage America.

At the American Lung Association office in Boston near the waterfront I was provided with a desk, part-time secretarial assistance, and an arrangement where I spent a full day in their offices once a week. It was one of the finest ongoing media consulting experiences of my career.

One of my most interesting smoking cessation awareness projects at the Lung Association was working with *Boston*

Globe cartoonist Paul Szep who had been the recipient of Pulitzers. He became our honorary Christmas Seal Campaign Chairman and filled that role with enthusiasm and creativity.

I was invited to Paul's studio located in the lower reaches of the *Globe* where he sat in a real barber's chair like the one my grandfather had used in his barber shop. He showed me how he raised and lowered it to suit his needs as an artist.

Based on Paul's brainstorm, we put together a series of TV public service messages using the Blue Danube Waltz. "Da da da da da um um...cough cough," I posed as one of the coughers puffing on a cigarette. This was the first time I had inhaled a cigarette since my own smoking years in my teens. And it was amazing how powerful that smoke was as it entered my throat and lungs. My cough was real.

For several years I was mass media consultant to Family Counseling & Guidance Centers which was headed by Monsignor Alves. They had a network of clinics in Boston and suburban areas. Considering the awful impact my mother's insanity had on my life, it was good for me to work with people dedicated to improving people's mental health.

The fund raising events sponsored by the Family Counseling agency were of the highest caliber. For example, a high ticket fund raising event held in the Natick area included gourmet dishes from places such as France and

Peru. The name of one dish was "tortured goose liver pate." The event was a high society extravaganza. So my public awareness campaign was easy to develop.

During my time with the agency, we were pioneers in providing public awareness for the problem of mood swings people often had after the Christmas Holidays. The post-Holiday blahs and blues. Year after year I was able to gather substantial media coverage on that subject as well as other psychological problems that coincided with seasons or holidays. I enjoyed that work.

Since God works in mysterious and fascinating ways, I also became a communications consultant to the central office of Catholic Charities serving Greater Boston. Life had taken me from childhood in a Catholic Charities group home to consultant for the agency overseeing the Catholic Charities in eastern Massachusetts.

Working with the agency's leaders, including Father O'Sullivan and Rev. Francis Irwin who later became a Bishop, my intuition suggested to me to keep my secret. This was not difficult for me because my early life had trained me in the art of secrecy about the facts of my existence.

Feeling a bit like a character in a Dickens novel with a secret origin, it was heartwarming to learn of the sincere dedication of the Catholic Charities staff to the well-being of the people they served.

Also, it was interesting to attract media coverage for Cardinal Medeiros' Garden Party, a lavish fund raiser. Located on the neatly manicured lawn in front of the humble Cardinal's palatial residence in Brighton, the prestigious event's attendance included the elite of Catholic society, and other community leaders prepared to give generously to the Cardinal's support for Catholic Charities.

My work with the central office of Catholic Charities led to other consulting opportunities with Catholic Charities agencies in Cambridge and north and south of Boston. It also provided some wisdom related to my habit of requiring annual contracts with my clients.

At one point I realized I was pricing my services too low and at contract time I confidently made a plea for a higher rate. Then I lost most of the agencies of Catholic Charities. They were on very tight budgets and were apparently shocked by my casual attempt to increase my income.

From then on I never used written contracts and that worked better. Also, the good news is that within a month of the loss of clients I had replaced them with other nonprofit organizations. Luckily, I was quickly able to fill the gap.

My years as an independent consultant with large and small agencies provided me with a continuing education in the world of health and human services. Those years also gave me many challenges in working with all kinds of people trying to serve others.

One of my most daunting tasks was meeting with two leaders who were developing a mission statement for a nonprofit organization related to addiction. We were a committee of three and what an endurance test it was to struggle with each word. Agreement was very elusive.

This reminds me of a comment to me by Ernie Henderson, the candid former President of Sheraton Corporation, who served on two different boards of directors connected with my work. "The best committee is a committee of three with one member home sick and another out of town on vacation."

As I move toward the end of this book, I am also reminded of another one of my favorite quotes provided by two anonymous women in England in the 1930s in the book titled *God Calling*: "Appreciation results from contrary experiences."

During my years of working with nonprofit organizations as their communications consultant I seldom had negative experiences. I enjoyed the work and considered it a blessing that instead of achieving my own Health Information Institute I was led into a reluctant role as communications consultant to health and human service agencies. My initial reluctance had soon been replaced by enthusiasm. The Lord functions with us in fascinating ways.

The work had ups and downs, as the title of this book indicates, but there is always a price to be paid for freedom. For me, the freedom to serve others as a specialist, not a staff executive or Chief Executive Officer, was worth the price.

Working in modern America as a freelance consultant had much in common with the role of a fisherman in the time of Jesus, and also in our time. One's way of life was not secure, not fixed. One was not in control.

I was subject to forces that could not be rationally understood. I had to constantly remind myself that the will of God must prevail, whether things were on the upswing to prosperity or on the way down into financial distress.

Family Challenges

Another kind of distress entered my life as 1980 opened. It was marital distress. As a result of differences that had become more and more irreconcilable I had made a decision to do something that had always terrified me when I had thought of it.

To understand myself better I entered psychoanalysis with a Jungian analyst who had been trained in Zurich at the Jung

Institute. His name was Joel Covitz, his Brookline office was near Boston University, and the analysis that he provided was a catalyst for major changes in my life.

We were able to discuss realities of my emotional life such as my mother's insanity that I had never shared with anybody else. To this day I use some of his advice and voice his actual words when I am faced with difficult decisions.

During this period I also became very moderate about my use of alcohol. I was getting more in touch with my own psyche and my physical, mental, emotional and spiritual needs. Paradoxically, the more I seemed to benefit from the nine months of Jungian psychoanalysis the more difficulty my wife and I were having.

Finally, early in 1981 my wife Mary and I separated, ending 27 years of marriage. Instead of growing together, we had grown apart, and had developed differences that could not be reconciled.

The separation and eventual divorce led to intense loneliness, serious financial challenges, adjustment to solitary living, and growth of new self-respect based on love of self and others.

At the time of the separation, my three daughters were young adults, but my son was only ten. He and I were very close and it was extremely difficult to be away from him and my young adult daughters on a day-to-day basis.

However, I stayed in touch with my daughters and I made it a point to spend quality time with my son. As the years passed, my visits to see him were consistent, unlike my own father's erratic connection with me, and we became dear friends as well as father and son.

The pain of divorce seemed almost unbearable at times, but we lived through it and grew emotionally. For me, the very idea of divorce had been unthinkable, but apparently it was necessary for me to experience it, as so many others have done.

The potential wealth from my real estate investments diminished rapidly. Before the marriage ended we owned a large home in Dedham with a very low mortgage, the house in Ogunquit, Maine with no mortgage, and I had half ownership in the old four-apartment tenement that had originally been the home of my grandparents.

If the marriage had remained intact, the future value of those properties was probably in the neighborhood of two million dollars. Instead, I moved into a period of rapid downward mobility and within a few years I was entirely without property.

I was destined to roam like a gypsy from apartment to apartment in Dedham, Canton, and on Cape Cod for more than fifteen years. That was an adventure in its own right. Finally, thanks to the G.I. Bill of Rights I became eligible to have my own house again here on the Cape in 1998.

As I leave my writing cave here and drive out of my driveway each day, if I turn my head to the right a bit I can see the sand dunes, beach house, and lifeguard station in the distance.

I could not ask for a better location and I have no complaints about the ups and downs I have experienced as a divorced Dad or as a freelance writer, author, lecturer, educator and communications consultant. I see it all as part of God's plan for the unfolding of my journey through life.

The way I see it, God is the author of the story of my life but he gives me free will to make some of my own decisions in the various chapters.

Freelance Writing and TV Production

My life as a freelance writer motivated me to become a member of the American Medical Writers Association (AMWA), and eventually I was elected President of the New England Chapter. Also, I served on the Board of Directors of the national organization. In addition, I served as President of Professional Writers of Cape Cod.

I attended AMWA conferences in various U.S. and

Canadian cities. At a conference in Toronto I was asked to present a session titled, "Launching a Freelance Writing Career." Based on that presentation I was invited to write a chapter on the same subject for the AMWA book *Biomedical Communication.*

One of the fascinating periods of my life as a freelance was during the early 1980s. I had my own public affairs show on Boston's Channel 25 when it was owned by the Christian Broadcasting Network.

For many years I had been a featured guest on just about every major radio and TV discussion show in the Boston and Eastern Massachusetts areas. Because I had felt comfortable as a guest the thought of having my own show entered my mind and motivated me to make a proposal.

After I conceived "It's Your Life," I visited a few media outlets with my package and finally got a show of interest in the Boston suburb of Needham at Channel 25 WXNE-TV. Then the Program Director told me, "We have to send your proposal to Virginia Beach for a decision."

A while later when I asked how the process was coming along, I was told, "We're waiting to hear from Virginia Beach." I wasn't sure whether Virginia was a lady or a place. Soon I learned that headquarters of Christian Broadcasting Network was at Virginia Beach, Virginia.

The show was approved, I got the green light, and we were launched based on this statement: "We'll try it for thirteen weeks." We produced two shows at a time twice a month and "It's Your Life" ran on Channel 25 every Sunday evening for nearly three years. It was a 30-minute public affairs show with no interruptions for commercials and I usually had just one guest. That was ideal for an interesting conversation.

Tim Robertson of Christian Broadcasting Network (CBN), televangelist Pat Robertson's son, directed the show for me in the early stages of his own career. I chose the guests and interviewed community leaders such as politicians, hospital presidents, authors, and spiritual leaders.

I enjoyed interviewing David DuPlessis, who was called "Mister Pentecost." On another show I interviewed Chaplain Ray about his prison ministry. I also had a number of chats with other dedicated Christians who carried the message of God's love. During those years I came to respect a large number of evangelical Christians who really meant it when they encouraged others with "Praise the Lord."

Most guests on my show rose to the occasion and provided a relaxed conversation. But there were some exceptions. One of the top officials in Massachusetts government was so self-centered that if I asked a question he would give a long speech instead of having a chat.

On the other hand there was an eminent psychiatrist who was so used to listening to clients that he tended to give uncomfortably brief responses to my questions. My aim with guests was to find the happy medium.

At the end of each show, as I was signing off I said, "Thank God for making this show possible." This was based on my belief that anything I do is only possible because of my Creator's decision to grant me the life I have lived.

My early work as a freelance led me to agencies such as the North Shore Council on Alcoholism, other councils on alcoholism, and Boston's Third Nail Drug Program. So I began to specialize in writing about the addictions.

I view the addictions as our world's major health problem leading to serious diseases of mind, body and spirit. I believe addictions are the idols that get between us and our Creator.

In 1983 I was visiting my lobbyist friend Tom Driscoll who was handling public affairs for Mount Pleasant Hospital, an addiction treatment center in Lynn, Mass. He gave me a copy of *The U.S. Journal of Drug & Alcohol Dependence* and said they seldom included information from the Northeast.

Tom suggested that I offer to be a freelance correspondent for the *Journal* in New England. I followed his advice and that fall they tested me with the assignment of covering a conference on alcoholism at Newport, Rhode Island. I was soon their National Correspondent in the northeast, writing feature articles each month to inform health professionals. I served in this capacity for eight years and I loved it.

My key function for the *Journal* was covering addiction conferences and reporting what the experts were saying. This was one of the most satisfying assignments during my freelance career.

I enjoyed listening at conference sessions, absorbing new information, and interviewing speakers. I also enjoyed the travel throughout New England and sometimes to Albany and New York City. This might have been classified as work but it often felt like a short vacation.

International Correspondent

On many occasions, my freelance writing combined work with pleasure. In 1984, one of these life-changing occasions was when I followed a suggestion by my mentor Mark Keller, a pioneer in the alcoholism field. Editor Emeritus of Rutgers' Journal of Alcohol Studies, Mark was a colleague of mine in the American Medical Writers Association.

Based on Mark's insistent prodding, I went to Israel for that nation's first international conference on alcoholism and the family. Shimon Peres, Minister for Labor, was keynote speaker. Attendees came from around the world.

Mark, a Bible scholar, was one of the presenters and while we were there he guided me around Jerusalem. With Mark as my guide, I had some experiences that would not be available to the average tourist.

Later, I wrote features about that conference for *The U. S. Journal of Drug and Alcohol Dependence* as well as for *Alcoholism Magazine* and other publications.

On the way to Israel I stopped at Rome for a few days. Former Governor John Volpe of Massachusetts sent a cable on my behalf to his friend Maxwell Rabb, U.S. Ambassador to Italy. A former Ambassador to Italy himself, Volpe asked Ambassador Rabb to help me in my quest for information.

As a result, I received V.I.P. treatment at the U.S. Embassy in Rome. The Embassy even provided me with an Italian interpreter who accompanied me. Then, as I played the part of international correspondent, I was given access to officials of the Italian government who could update me on drug and alcohol problems in that country.

After that, I visited a drug treatment program next to the River Tiber. This gave me more material for feature stories that were published later.

Before returning home after the conference in Israel I

spent some time in Egypt which turned out to be an astounding mystical experience. Later I did some travel writing about my experiences in Italy, Israel and Egypt.

Another example of combining business and pleasure was my 1985 trip to the University of Stirling at Edinburgh, Scotland. This was a special assignment from the Rev. David Works. I covered a conference stimulated by his North Conway Institute, an addiction ministry located in Boston.

The conference was about alcoholism in the workplace and was hosted by the Church of Scotland. Among other adventures, I visited the Simpson House where pioneering experiments in anesthesia had taken place. Also, I was invited to observe the colorful "haggis" ceremony.

In addition to the writing I did for the North Conway Institute, I was able to write about that Scottish conference for the *U.S. Journal of Drug and Alcohol Dependence*.

While attending the conference in Scotland I met a health professional from Sweden who surprised me by telling me he was familiar with my writing in the *U.S. Journal*. We writers don't know how far our words will travel.

Before returning home, I made my first visit to Ireland where I interviewed experts and gathered additional material for freelance articles on Irish alcoholism.

As time passed, I wrote for such publications as *The*

Journal of the Addiction Research Foundation in Toronto and the *Medical Post*, another Canadian publication.

In *Catholic Digest* I wrote feature stories on the lives of Boston's Cardinal Medeiros and "The Junkie Priest," Father Dan Egan, who was not a junkie himself but helped many addicts. I interviewed him at the Graymoor monastery in upstate New York near the Hudson River.

Working in the addiction field led me to take a close look at my own use of alcohol and valium. Therefore, I decided in 1983 to abstain from alcohol and other drugs. It was a healthy decision. Since then I have not found it necessary to consume mind altering substances. That has left my mind free for God to do any altering that needed to be done.

Every portion of my life has been part of a mosaic of sorts, often misunderstood by me, but important in God's master plan for my spiritual development. If, as Shakespeare said, life is a stage on which we are the players, I have played opposite parts a number of times.

I have been a married man and a divorced person, factory worker and CEO, subordinate and leader, voter and elected official, loser in elections and winner of elections, student and professor, poor and well off, renter and property owner, participant in accidents and accident prevention leader, a person terrified of public speaking and a professional lecturer, a talk show guest and a talk show host, a borderline agnostic and an enthusiastic believer.

I have had a vast and varied set of experiences during this time on Earth that we call "life." I am not boasting; I'm simply passing on the truth. Through God's grace I have had many dreams come true, in workplaces and other places. Nevertheless, the most amazing event in my life was not directly related to work. Instead, it was related to my spiritual journey.

In spiritual development, the ability to endure and then enjoy solitude is very important. As I look back on my life, I can see that it was necessary for me to spend long periods living alone during the years leading to my spiritual enlightenment at Peterborough, New Hampshire, in the Monadnock Mountains on September 5, 1985.

If the spiritual aspects of my life interest you, I encourage you to get a copy of *The Monadnock Revelations: A Spiritual Memoir* which provides the details of my journey. Also, a brief summary of how I channeled the voice of God is outlined at my website sanctuary777.com.

Since September 5, 1985 I have been leading somewhat of a double life as a man who has experienced God directly through "cosmic consciousness" and a person pursuing an apparently ordinary life as a freelance writer, professional lecturer, and educator.

The Freelance Writer on Cape Cod

Shortly after my enlightening spiritual experience that September, I moved to Cape Cod. My first day on the Cape was Columbus Day, October 12, 1985. Like Columbus, I believed I knew where I was going, and I did not know what would happen when I got there.

I had very few Boston area clients when I moved to Cape Cod. But I soon attracted an arrangement with Monomoy Community Services, a mental health agency headquartered in Chatham on the Cape. That organization was my first Cape Cod client. I soon got more.

Also, I continued my affiliation with the Cape Cod Writers' Conference which later evolved into the Cape Cod Writers' Center. I served on the Board of Directors and was part-time Program Director for the Center for a year or so. I had the pleasure of introducing humorist Art Buchwald at the Annual Conference.

Before moving to the Cape I had been the only off-Cape member of a group called The Twelve O'Clock Scholars. An offshoot of the Conference, the Scholars met twice a month in homes throughout the Cape. When I took up residence on Cape Cod I continued my membership in this group where we read to each other from our writing "in progress."

During one of these meetings another member suggested that I utilize my writing for *The U.S. Journal of Drug and Alcohol Dependence* and make a proposal to the *Cape Cod Times* about doing a weekly column on the addictions.

By the time January 1986 arrived I was writing a weekly column, "On Addiction," for the *Times* on the Advice page in an excellent spot next to Ann Landers.

The editor, Bill Breisky, had said, "Do four columns and we'll try it for a month and see how it goes." For the next thirteen years my column appeared each Thursday, reaching between 50,000 and in excess of 100,000 readers, depending on how many tourists were in the area. So I had an audience for my insights into addiction and spirituality.

Bill Breisky told me that my column was one of his favorites. However, a while after he retired, the new editor who replaced Bill at the *Cape Cod Times* dropped my column. C'est la vie. "Freelance" doesn't mean "permanent."

Nevertheless, I was able to continue the addiction theme for a while in a health/lifestyle column for the *Cape Cod Journal*, the first online daily newspaper in America, which advertised that it was "ahead of the *Times*." I guess it was too far ahead because it went out of business due to a dearth of advertising revenue.

This was followed by five years of writing my addiction column on a monthly basis for *The Cape Codder*. In the end, I had written newspaper columns on the Cape for 20 years when I called it a day and concentrated on lecturing and publishing my own books via Sanctuary Unlimited.

I was led into writing about the addictions in the Boston area and when I became a columnist on the Cape I accepted my destiny as an addiction specialist. While I was getting more involved in the development of my own spirituality, the addiction writing became a nice fit.

Increasing my understanding of addiction, I served for a while as a group facilitator at Cape Counseling Center in Hyannis, working with alcoholics who had been assigned by the courts to an advanced alcohol education program. In that role I was able to encourage abstinence and spiritual growth through Twelve Step Program participation.

Baptism by Fire

Another aspect of spiritual growth entered my life during my second Holiday Season on Cape Cod. I had been invited to attend a lady's Christmas gathering but could not make it, so she arranged for me to come the following evening. She said she would save me some cookies and preserve what was left of the candles on her tree.

She was using live candles, and as a safety crusader I had given presentations on Boston TV about the hazards of such practices. But I accepted the invitation. When the candles were lit for a while she resisted my counsel to snuff them out. And soon the dry tree went up in terrifying flames.

There was no fire extinguisher available. Running into a bedroom, I grabbed a quilt for smothering the flames but she screamed that the quilt was an heirloom and wouldn't let me use it. By the time I had gotten a bed spread and run back to the tree with it, the flames were licking the ceiling of the very expensive home which resembled an upscale museum of art with its white rugs and valuable artifacts.

I tried to smother the flames with the bed spread but it just levitated from the intense heat. The flaming house was rapidly emptied of oxygen. Then I felt my lungs shutting down and within seconds my lungs stopped functioning.

I told her breathlessly that we had to get out fast. When we reached the front yard the house was an inferno. Later she gave me credit for saving our lives, but the credit was not mine. It belonged to the Lord who directed my actions.

One of her two poodles came outside with us. The other ran to a bedroom and died there. The lady's arms had burns from her attempts to deal with the flaming tree. My coat and leather cap were burned to a crisp in her front closet.

Soon the ambulance arrived and so did the fire trucks. To allow smoke to exit, holes were chopped in the roof. The front picture window was purposely smashed. Burned objects were heaved into a huge pile on the front lawn. By a small miracle, I found my key case there. It held my house and car keys and was scorched. The house was a total loss.

My mind was crisp and clear during the whole event but post-traumatic stress affected my breathing for several days afterward. I think part of that problem was related to my asthma and my body's memory of the nearly fatal lung collapse I had experienced when I was six months old.

I came out of the harrowing experience with the house fire having great gratitude for my presence of mind during the conflagration. I thanked the Lord for that. But every time since then when I have been in a home using live candles I recall that Holiday fire. PTSD gets me apprehensive.

I also remember other occasions when I came close to departing from this planet. I am grateful to the Lord for protecting me and guiding me through many dangers so that I may continue my spiritual journey. I believe this journey of life is for the soul, not the body. But we need our bodies.

The spiritual journey is very relevant to addiction recovery. After all, the addictions that afflict us are what I consider to be the idol worship that has always been a challenge for the human condition in the battle between good and evil, the struggle between the light and the darkness.

In my own voluntary work at Cape Cod Community Media Center on this subject, I produced more than twenty 30-minute videos with the title "Understanding Addiction." Essentially, this was a condensation of the information in my book *Addicted? A Guide to Understanding Addiction*.

Freelance Writer and Professor

After teaching courses at New Hampshire College while living in Maine, the idea of doing more college level teaching hovered in the back of mind. So when I was settled on Cape Cod for a while I filed an employment application at Cape Cod Community College.

Nothing happened at first, but then one day in the spring of 1988 I saw a classified ad in the Cape Cod Times that interested me. The College was looking for an instructor in a satellite program at Plymouth that summer for women on welfare who were making the transition back to work.

The program needed a math instructor and an English instructor. I was selected to be the English instructor and that experience with the satellite program led to a part-time faculty position at the main campus in West Barnstable.

So, in the fall of 1988 I became an adjunct English

Professor at Cape Cod Community College, a member of the faculty in the Language and Literature Department. An "adjunct" is a part-timer who has to sign a separate contract for each semester's assignment. A professional "temp."

During this period, in addition to teaching some writing courses I taught a community services course in addiction based on my book *Addicted? A Guide to Understanding Addiction.* Later, I offered a success course and a course in healthy relating which is important in addiction recovery. That course was based on my book *Improving Intimacy: 10 Powerful Strategies~A Spiritual Approach.*

This gave me the opportunity to mention spirituality often because addiction can be considered a "soul sickness" and a spiritual disease even though it also has physical and mental aspects. The most effective recoveries that I know about are those based on having a spiritual awakening through participation in an A.A. Twelve Step recovery group.

Not long after arriving on Cape Cod I was fortunate to attract a client that kept me busy for several years. At Beech Hill Hospital in Dublin, New Hampshire, I served as their communications consultant and handled their mass media needs. Also, I was Editor of their "News" publication that circulated to many thousands of Beech Hill alumni and a large number of professionals in the addiction field.

It was an ideal freelance assignment with an excellent hourly rate and the pleasure of doing my writing and editing at my home office in Dennisport on Cape Cod where I sat at my TRS-80 computer/word processor in a rented condo with an ocean view of Nantucket Sound. I handled interviews of Beech Hill personnel by phone and in one-on-one sessions during my monthly visits to the hospital's site atop a small mountain in the Monadnock area at Dublin, New Hampshire.

Beech Hill was a pioneering addiction treatment center that practiced state-of-the-art psychology and a whole range of therapies, including the Outward Bound wilderness experience for recovering teens. These offerings were blended with a Twelve Step approach to recovery.

Part of my work with Beech Hill Hospital involved a visit to Thompson's Island in Boston Harbor to attend a smaller version of the Outward Bound experience. I was there to write about it and take some photos.

The day's events centered on a seminar for therapists. The seminar was very interesting and I developed a lengthy summary of the remarks for my client.

Later, when I was outside watching a group exercise in a large field, about fifty or sixty folks formed a large circle, each one behind another person. When somebody suggested that I join the circle I made the mistake of saying yes.

The game was to keep compressing the circle. Each person was expected to scrunch up behind another person and keep shrinking the circle until it broke and people went flying. Who was I to question the process?

As I stood there I wondered what would happen if the circle broke at my point. There was a huge man right in front of me and my vision of what could happen was not a pleasant one. I did not wish to be crushed.

Well, the circle broke and everybody went flying. The huge man in front of me collapsed onto my body and it felt as if my hip was breaking. I limped for the rest of that day and when I visited my chiropractor the next day he said I was very lucky that the man hadn't fallen onto my hip an inch or two from the injured area. My hip would have been completely crushed.

Since that time I have been much more cautious about which invitations I accept or pass up. That helps me keep my body in one piece.

The assignment with Beech Hill lasted until the recession of 1990-1991 during which the health care sector was hit very hard. Also, I was hit with great impact. More than half my monthly income came from that facility.

On a wintry visit to Beech Hill I was invited into Vice President Sally Morgan's office where I heard a comment I will always remember: "Tom, we're going to have to curtail your activities after you complete your current work."

On that weekend there was a severe snowstorm that made driving very hazardous. While I was motoring up the steep mountain to attend an evening seminar I was going to write about, the Volvo had a tough time getting traction. The road was unplowed. Visibility was poor. No guard rails existed.

The snow kept falling, and later in the evening as I drove back down the narrow mountain road with its sharp turns my goal was to safely reach Beech Hill Lodge where I was staying overnight. I almost didn't get there because halfway down my car went out of control and began to spin in circles.

Remembering the advice I had once given people over the air waves when I was an accident prevention crusader, I avoided hitting the brakes hard, tapped them very lightly instead, and held the steering wheel lightly.

With time standing still, I spun around in complete circles seven or eight times before coming to a stop at the edge of a steep drop into a deep valley in the forest.

I was the only car on the mountain at that time. Therefore, if I had dropped over the edge of the road there would have been no sign of my exit. It was a very close call that I will never forget.

Taking a deep breath, I thanked the Lord for guiding me

into safety, and then I crept very slowly down the perilous grade to my refuge at the lodge.

The next morning when I mentioned my skidding adventure to the woman overseeing the lodge she just shook her head and made a remark about the chances some people take under adverse conditions. Without saying it directly, she must have considered me to be a demented driver.

The following months brought a very serious exercise in downward mobility. I have said that Beech Hill provided more than half my monthly income. Well, I needed that income to meet obligations. But now I was nearly flat broke.

To survive the income gap, I had to use multiple credit cards with various banks and I rapidly plunged deeper and deeper into debt. At one point my income was so low that I decided to apply for food stamps.

After going through all the red tape that the welfare system entails, I was told that my monthly income was 100 dollars too high to qualify. This was very frustrating.

I started scraping up any money I could get from just about any available job. For two summers I worked at Ocean Edge resort in Brewster on Cape Cod for $5.50 an hour checking people's passes as they entered the swimming pool.

If it rained I didn't work and this lowered my weekly income substantially. The pay of $5.50 an hour for a couple of days each week didn't go very far. At Beech Hill Hospital my hourly rate had been more than thirty dollars an hour.

On the positive side, during my downtime at the pool I was able to read Melville's *Moby Dick* masterpiece slowly. Also, I read some other magnificent literature including *Narcissus & Goldmund* by Herman Hesse.

In addition, I had the amazing experience of seeing the nuptial flight of the queen bee a couple of times. After copulating in a dramatic mid-air struggle, the queen and her consort fell to the ground. Then the satisfied queen took a few deep breaths, got up, stretched, and happily flew away. The consort shuddered a few times and then died.

During this period I tried to find additional freelance writing to do, but the marketplace had dried up. It was one of those rare times when all of my attempts to find work failed.

No matter where I turned, work eluded me. No longer did I have the situation where I would leave one job on a Friday and start a new one the following Monday. I was blocked.

On one occasion I answered an ad for secretarial work because I could always type better than most of the secretaries I had hired. The Assembly of Delegates on Cape Cod had me do a typing test and I passed with flying colors.

But even though I had de-emphasized some of the highly successful parts of my resume, I was told that if I got the job

I probably wouldn't stay there long because of all the high level positions I had held. So they did not offer me the secretarial position. I had to agree with their logic. But the feeling of being virtually unemployable because I was overqualified was difficult to relate to.

One of the results of that recession for me was the need to do something I had always considered unacceptable. I had to declare bankruptcy. I had always been a person proud of his credit rating. And bankruptcy would destroy my rating.

The other item I had considered unacceptable until the early 1980s was divorce. Therefore, now I had been forced by circumstances to perform both of the actions I had been so biased against for many years.

After all, why should I escape divorce and bankruptcy? Compassion is achieved when one has to walk in somebody else's shoes. No longer did I make judgments about divorced people or those who had experienced bankruptcy. Sometimes humility is gained by being humiliated.

Because I had no desire to become a full-time Professor, it was with some reluctance that I began teaching additional courses at Cape Cod Community College. Soon, by necessity, I was carrying almost a full-time load of three English courses plus some community service courses.

Unfortunately, this began to feel like the kind of full-time work I had become allergic to. So it was a challenge for me, especially when I taught two sections of the same course. I would find myself repeating the same joke to a class, handing out Xeroxes I had already given them, or commenting on an assignment I had already covered. I had never been adept at repetitive functions. I preferred variety.

In 1991 I also took on a 20-hours-a-week job at the College as a writing coach, mentor, and academic advisor for occupational education students in the Coaches & Mentors Program. So I had to reduce my teaching of English courses.

Both the part-time teaching position plus the tutoring and advising for the Coaches & Mentors Program were destined to run for about 20 years. But I didn't think this conflicted with my pledge never to stay in the same full-time occupation more than five years. After all, I was part-time faculty, not full-time. And the tutoring/advising was part of a grant program that could be ended just about any time.

Lectures, Books and Social Security

With the passage of time and advancing senior citizen status, I moved away from communications consulting and concentrated on my own writing while teaching and tutoring writing at Cape Cod Community College.

In 1994, at age 62, I joined the millions of people enrolled in the Social Security retirement system which I had paid into since age 14 when I got my first Social Security ID card while caddying at Saranac Inn in upper New York State.

This new source of monthly income eased some of my financial pressure. However, the transition was a difficult exercise in downward mobility. To meet my obligations, I needed to exceed the income limits set by the Social Security system. This meant that for my first two years in the program I had to pay back about $2,500 a year out of my earnings.

An official at Social Security made it clear to me after I had used the word "penalty" that I was not paying a penalty. I was simply "paying back" money I should not have received from Social Security. That was the reality. Hey, who ever said life transitions should be easy?

In recent years I have moved away from my work in higher education at the community college. I have gradually adjusted to my status as a basically "retired" person.

Actually, I have never believed in retirement as a way of life. And when people have asked, "Are you retired?" I would quip, "No, I'm not retired; I'm just tired."

I chose not to work toward a pension or a life without creative work. The only one of my employers that had even offered a pension plan was Amica. I was not interested.

My main focus these days is writing and publishing my

own books, a true not-for-profit arrangement due to printing and other costs. Also, I do some talks for community groups, libraries and others who appreciate my writing.

Years ago, in this age of digital writing and reproduction, I shifted my focus not only to writing my books but also to building my own website sanctuary777.com. The 200 essays there on addiction and recovery are a public service for those who wish to learn more about addiction.

At the end of this book you will find a list of the books I have written and published under my imprint of Sanctuary Unlimited. My books are available through any bookseller.

I am very grateful to the following helpful booksellers on Cape Cod: Booksmith/Musicsmith in Orleans, Books by the Sea in Osterville, Market Street Books at Mashpee Commons, and the Keltic Kottage in West Yarmouth.

As a public service, I am now in the process of producing a series of programs on Cape Cod's public access channel 99 for the ten books I have published. And I will soon have most of my books available on Kindle.

To lead a balanced life and mingle with others away from the cottage "cave" where I write, I maintain my affiliations with Cape Cod Writers Center, New England Chapter of the American Medical Writers Association, A Book in the Hand, Irish American Club of Cape Cod, Boston College Alumni

Association, and Boston University Alumni Network.

In addition, I am a member of the Roman Catholic Church, the Secular Franciscan Order, and Twelve Step "anonymous" mutual help groups. Also, I participate in a group known as The Media Gang comprised of veterans of Massachusetts TV, Radio and other media outlets.

Often I leave my cave to drive to the Barnes & Noble store at the Cape Cod Mall for a cup of tea or coffee and a bagel. I enjoy the change of scene and the opportunity to browse through various books on the shelves.

Among my favorite books there are Anton Chekhov's short stories and biographies of Winston Churchill. I recently purchased *Forty Ways to Look at Winston Churchill* by Gretchen Rubin and I am enjoying it greatly.

Why Churchill? My Irish Granny used to curse him this way: "The dirty blackguard Winnie, may his immortal soul rot in hell forever...God forgive me for saying it." From her point of view, any British politician was an enemy.

Actually, Winnie was helpful in Ireland's quest for independence. Besides, I appreciate his wit, his intelligence, his courageous battle with depression, and his indomitable spirit in the face of ridicule and fierce opposition. More than that, he was an expert at upward and downward mobility.

As I look back on my work life in this 11th book I can

clearly see how lucky I have been through the years to find useful and creative work while being part of a loving family, relating to an abundance of good friends and colleagues, and pursuing writing goals near and dear to my heart.

Along the way, some very pleasant surprises have come my way. One of them was *Cape Cod Life Magazine's* selection of me in their 25th Anniversary issue as "one of the top 100 influential people" on Cape Cod. The factor that made this especially pleasant was that I did not seek this recognition. It came as a complete surprise to me.

As I have noted before, everything else in my life pales before the gift of spiritual enlightenment and cosmic consciousness the Lord gave me in a direct encounter on September 5, 1985. So I have no need to complain about any challenges that life poses for me. I simply view the hurdles as part of God's will for one of His messengers.

As I have reviewed my upward and downward mobility and zigzag work life it has become increasingly clear to me that the hand of God has been involved in every moment of my life through direct intervention or God's permission. And life itself on a daily basis has been an ongoing gift.

As I introduced myself to you in the opening pages of this memoir, I mentioned the MMPI personality inventory which tagged me with the following descriptions:

- Highly rebellious and nonconformist
- Touchy, sensitive
- Artistic, bohemian temperament
- Confused feelings, moody
- Moderately depressed, worrying
- Restless or agitated

These were some of the factors that helped shape my life as an employee, a boss, and my own boss. Looking back on my work life, I think it has been an interesting adventure. I hope it has interested you too.

Also, I look forward to more adventures, especially the trip to Nepal to see what the Lord has written in a monastery there. Obviously, I will need guidance about which monastery to visit and it will take a large chunk of money to finance my expedition. But I trust that the Lord will provide.

Now I am leaving you with a few more quotes from *God Calling* by A.J. Russell, one of my favorite spiritual books. "Love and laugh." "Fear not, all is well." "Never feel inadequate for any task." "Appreciation results from contrary experience." "Be still, be calm." "Go forward unafraid."

What a journey life is! What an adventure! What a piece of work! I wish you joy in your own work and fulfillment in your journey through life. It's your life. God bless you.

About the Author

The 25th Anniversary issue of *Cape Cod Life Magazine* selected Tom as "one of the top 100 influential people" on Cape Cod. Also, he is listed in *Who's Who in the East*.

Tom is a Cape Cod Writer and Lecturer. Take a look at his **sanctuary777.com** website where you will find many essays as well as excerpts from his books.

A Few Facts

Bachelor of Arts *cum laude*. History & Government.
Boston College, College of Arts & Sciences.
Also, advanced Graduate Study at Boston College.

Master of Arts. History. (U.S. and European).
Boston University,
Graduate School of Arts & Sciences.

Served as Dedham (Mass.) School Committee Chairman, Town Meeting Member, Political Campaign Organizer, Lobbyist at the State House on Beacon Hill in Boston.

Formerly the CEO of four different organizations: Chevrolet Dealers Association, Boston Public Housing Tenants Policy Council, Massachusetts Federation of Nursing Homes, Massachusetts Safety Council.

Independent Freelance Writer & Editor since 1978.

Publisher, *Lifestyle Journal* at www.sanctuary777.com.

His website provides excerpts from his books and some 200 lifestyle essays emphasizing addiction and recovery.

Past President, American Medical Writers Association, New England Chapter. Member (1980-   ).

English Professor, Adjunct Faculty,
Cape Cod Community College (1988-2007).

Writing Tutor/Mentor/Advisor,
Cape Cod Community College (1991-2010).

Member, Cape Cod Writers' Center (1981-   ).
Served as Board member and Program Planner.

National Correspondent, *U.S. Journal of Drug & Alcohol Dependence* (1983-1991).

Columnist, *Cape Cod Times* (1986-1999).

Columnist, *Cape Cod Journal* (1999-2000).

Columnist, *The Cape Codder* (2000-2005).

Affiliated with A Book in the Hand at Sears Library.

Political Commentator, campaign2america.com

Member, Secular Franciscan Order (1980-   )

Sanctuary Unlimited Books

Upward & Downward Mobility:
A Work Memoir (A Writer's Zigzag Journey)
By Tom O'Connell 64,000 words 1930s to 2012

In a candid, informal style, writer Tom O'Connell traces his work life from his early days in the 1930s and 1940s as an orphan in a Catholic Charities group home upward to top leadership roles in Massachusetts. He recalls challenging careers as CEO, educator, writer, columnist, host of public affairs show "It's Your Life" on Boston's Channel 25.

People known nationally and locally emerge in this book: Victor Borge, John Volpe, Mike Dukakis, Dick Flavin, Paul Szep, Frank Sargent, Kevin White, Dapper O'Neil.

The memoir takes the reader on a roller coaster ride of job searches and major achievements as he moves upward from Granny's house next to the railroad tracks to appointment to the Governor's Highway Safety Committee, CEO of Massachusetts Safety Council, inclusion in *Who's Who in the East*, and selection in *Cape Cod Life's* 25th Anniversary Issue as "one of the top 100 influential people" on Cape Cod.

From heights of upward mobility and success, O'Connell also reveals periods when he plummeted from those heights into times of downward mobility when faced with divorce, illness, bankruptcy and other serious challenges.

"Tom re-creates the 'Anything is Possible' myth of American culture after World War II."
--**W. A. Cole, Book Reviewer**

"This is more than a lone wolf's professional journal. His long time readers know Tom's independent thinking and deep faith. It's the story of a soul who will not sacrifice his values."
--**Dr. Finbarr Corr, Author, Former Priest, Therapist, Professor**

"Tom's memoirs are written like novels."
--**Jordan Rich, *WBZ News Radio* 1030, Boston.**

Deviant Shelter:
Year Three of The New Social System (NSS)
A Novel

It is Year Three of The New Social System (NSS) and all mental health institutions, prisons and correctional facilities in the United Econocratic Provinces have been replaced with deviant shelters for those who do not fit the government's current definition of the word "normal."

Doctor Wylie Fayne, a philosophy Professor, is the first resident of a new psychological deviant shelter with highly advanced technology. He is housed in a triangular-shaped unit in the Total Scrutiny Wing of the granite shelter constructed as a pyramid.

The Professor has the distinction of being the first to experience the new Time Void Therapy. Neuropsychological implants (NPI) have been attached to his nervous system. The goal of his therapy is to move him toward an acceptable mental condition so he can be useful to the government.

"**Engaging...reminiscent of James Joyce, George Orwell, Franz Kafka...unique vision of 21st Century...a dark sense of humor.**"—W.A. Cole, Book Reviewer. "A vivid imagination...It's so different...I was impressed."—Bob Silverberg, *Books & The World* TV. ($17)

Power, Politics & Propaganda:
Observations of a Curious Contrarian

This collection of thought-provoking essays is a reminder about the importance of individual liberty in a world moving toward more systems of government putting the group first.

O'Connell explores how power, politics and propaganda lead to supremacy of the collective over the free individual.

The danger, he contends, is that despite allegedly good intentions the elite collectivists and secularists are apt to consider those who believe in God as candidates for the Flat Earth Society.

O'Connell's key philosophy: "Individual liberty is our birthright...Respect for life is the key to both individual liberty and group harmony."

He says a Divine Plan is at work in the destinies of individuals and nations. Unimpressed with mob dynamics, he stresses individual liberty.

"You are really pointing the pathway here."--Bob Silverberg, *Books & The World* TV. "I thoroughly enjoyed your eye opening and thought-provoking book...It's a great read."—Jack Coffey, retired entrepreneur. "O'Connell's book is political prophecy."—W.A. Cole, Book Reviewer. ($17)

Bugging Out: An Army Memoir (1954)
With wit and irony, the author uses candid dialogue and vivid descriptions to tell how he dealt with the military assaults on his independent personality.

As a "voluntary" draftee with a pregnant wife, he is demoralized by cruel superiors and caught between duty and self-preservation. Reluctantly, he turns to "bugging out" as he tries to cope with the Army's challenges to his sanity.

His memoir provides memories of his adventures as a military misfit. Scenes reflect outrage, despair, and hilarity.

"Very vivid...a fascinating read."—Bob Silverberg, *Books & The World* TV. **"A real picture of what it was like...no holds barred."**--*Provincetown Banner*. **"A let-it-all-hang-out memoir...interesting characters."**-*Barnstable Patriot*. ($17)

The O'Connell Boy: Educating "The Wolf Child" ~ An Irish-American Memoir (1932-1950)
Lively impressions of a "wolf child" life in homes with solitary Irish immigrant women. Nine years at Mrs. White's "lace curtain Irish" Catholic Charities group home with her perfectionist "reign of terror." Then a "free" teen's "battle of wits" with Irish granny on "the other side of the tracks."

"Tom O'Connell connects with readers soul to soul...inspires."--Jordan Rich, *WBZ News Radio* 1030, Boston. **"a page-turner...heart wrenching...stunning."**--*Cape Cod Magazine*. **"a fascinating memoir...a charming and honest writing voice."**--*The Cape Codder*. **"O'Connell writes compellingly..."**--*Cape Cod Times*. **"compelling and inspiring."**--*Barnstable Patriot*. ($17)

Improving Intimacy: 10 Powerful Strategies
~A Spiritual Approach
A look at spiritually based intimacy, addictive relating, control, listening, communication, conflict. 10 strategies for healthy, loving relationships.

"Positive...powerful...very readable style."--*Cape Cod Times*. "It's the finest example of anyone writing on this subject."--Don LaTulippe, WPLM, Plymouth. ($10)

The Odd Duck: A Story for Odd People of All Ages
A cheerful, inspiring fable for "adult children." A lost duck raised in a chicken coop feels odd. After an identity crisis, a quest for self-worth brings healthy, lasting love.

"A cheerful, punning little allegory mostly for grownups."--*Bostonia Magazine*. "a parable for spiritual reawakening."--*Seniors Cape Cod Forum*. ($10)

Danny The Prophet: A Fantastic Adventure
A man reluctant to be God's last prophet has more worldly plans. A fantastic journey: a politician, a sage, an angel, many perilous adventures, divine revelations.

Readers' say: "Astounding!" "Wow!" "Funny!" "A wonderful book!" "A pleasure to read!" ($17)

The Monadnock Revelations: A Spiritual Memoir
The true story of Tom's mystical journey. A special hour with God in the Monadnock Mountains. A report on Cosmic Consciousness. Divine revelations.
   Readers' comments: "Encourages, energizes and inspires..." "It warmed my heart and inspired my soul." "A treasury of inspiration." "I loved it!" "Extremely visionary, well written, inspiring...a great book." ($17)

Addicted?: A Guide to Understanding Addiction
A practical guide toward greater understanding of the addictions. Alcohol, drugs, gambling, relationships, etc.
   "A wealth of information ...highly readable" --Blaise Gambino, Ph.D., Director of Research & Education, Gambling Program, Harvard Medical School. ($17)

Up In Smoke: The Nicotine Challenge in Recovery
Nearly 20,000 of these motivational booklets originally published by Hazelden were used in smoking cessation programs to help recovering alcoholics to also quit smoking. Hazelden has returned all rights to the author. ($10)

Note:

When ordering directly from sanctuary777.com, pay by check and add $5 to each price for shipping and handling.

To use credit card, go to any bookseller

To order books, refer your bookseller to
Ingram Book Company
or place your order through sanctuary777.com

Thank you!

Your comments on this book will be much appreciated!

email: info@sanctuary777.com, Website: sanctuary777.com
PO Box 25, Dennisport, MAssachusetts 02639, USA

NOTES